Have you ever played "What i

I have; more times than . ᴗᴗᴗᴗ ᴗᴗᴜᴜ. What if I'd gone ahead and joined the Air Force? What if I'd never worked for Park City? What if Aunt Ruth had never helped save Dennis Lynn Rader's Life?

Oh boy…that last one is a BIG "What if?" Here's how it happened.

The construction crew was nearing completion of the new addition at the back of City Hall. One night they left a propane heater running inside the unfinished area. I think they did this to keep the mudding on the sheet rock from getting too cold.

As usual, Dennis showed up to work way before anyone else, probably about 7:30, a half-hour early. So, he caught the full brunt of the carbon monoxide. He was slumped over his desk when Aunt Ruth, Deputy City Clerk for Water Service, and Sylvia, who also worked there, walked past the open door to our little office. One of them asked, "Dennis …Dennis…are you all right?"

He raised himself a bit and mumbled, "I need to sit for a while…" Then he slumped again and closed his eyes.

Aunt Ruth and Sylvia grabbed him and dragged him out of the building. A little longer and he probably would have died.

Some time after Dennis was arrested I asked her, "How do you and Sylvia feel about helping the BTK killer out of his office and saving his life?"

"Oh my gosh, I forgot all about that," my aunt replied, her face flushing red.

Although I didn't voice it, I wondered if I should grab her and shake her every now and then just to remind her of what she'd done.

UCS PRESS PMB 119
1702 W. Camelback Rd. # 13
Phoenix, AZ 85015

UCS PRESS is an imprint of MarJim Books, Inc.

Contact publisher regard quantity orders at
ordering@marjimbooks.com

Editor: James E. Porter, Sr.

Cover design by Marty Dobkins

Cover photo used by arrangement with AP Images.

Printed in the United States of America

First edition, first printing, June 2007

ISBN: 978-0-943247-09-0

Author's Note

For six-and-one-half years I worked as a Compliance Officer for the City of Park City, Kansas, issuing citations to people not in compliance with city codes; everything from loose dogs to trashy yards to inoperable vehicles; anything that was not considered a criminal issue—the police handled that.

Park City is a bedroom community of about 5,500 nestled against the northern boundary of Wichita, Kansas. I don't know how many times people have asked me, "Why didn't you just leave?"

It was mainly people asking this question after February 25, 2005 when the world found out my boss was the BTK killer.

Gotta admit it is a logical question in the minds of the askers. But none of them wore my shoes. They didn't get divorced from a member of the City Council, remarry only to have that marriage annulled under false pretense, have a brother commit suicide, and constantly worry about losing the insurance coverage I had if I quit...all while under the work supervision of a man whose aura of evil gradually enveloped me, wearing me down mentally and physically.

My frequent complaints about Dennis Rader's behavior toward me and my pleas for help were ignored. After all, my supervisor was a leader in his church and had worked with the Cub Scouts. "He's just being Dennis."

Hell, him "just being Dennis" nearly destroyed my life. Just a few days before I wrote this *Author's Note* I had another nightmare. This time he escaped from prison and was trying to kill me, and no one would believe me. I awoke in a dripping sweat, trying desperately to clear my head, making sure it was a dream and not really happening.

I felt I'd be damned if I left my job; damned if I stayed. I chose the latter damnation by rationalizing that at least I'd have health coverage.

I truly was Dennis Rader's next victim even if he never physically abused, tortured, and strangled me. As you will find out in this book, there are very valid reasons for me to believe that he was indeed considering me as a future *project* as he called his murder victims.

Mary Capps
May 18, 2007

Dedication

To those whose families and friends were victims of Dennis Radar: may evil never touch your lives again.

In memory

Jeffery Capps

February 23, 1970 – December 3, 2000

Acknowledgments

To my daughter Krissy, and sons Corporal Kyle Lloyd USMC and Trenton Lloyd—my three biggest allies; parents George and Violet Capps, for their unconditional love and support; brother Hobert, for his great listening ear; sister Kim Simon for her support; and sister, best friend, confidante, Michelle Wood. Also, to Dan Lickey, Rod Northcutt, and Bob Campbell; to Aunt Janice for taking up the cause and fighting City Hall; to many aunts, uncles, cousins, as well as friends; to Jim and Marty Dobkins, who helped make this book possible; to my brother Jeff, whose memory gives me comfort; and to Jim Mies for his love and understanding.

My boss was the BTK killer

I was the next victim

Mary Capps with Jim Dobkins

About Mary's co-author

Jim Dobkins is a Southwest-based writer. His co-author credits include *Winnie Ruth Judd: The Trunk Murders*, *Machine-Gun Man*, and *The Ararat Conspiracy*. He conceptualized and wrote the dramatized short *Someone Who Cares*. He has ghostwritten several books. Upcoming co-author releases include a revisit of the Judd murder case, a celebrity death investigative book, and two inspirational books—*He made moccasins*, and *Walking on the dead*. He co-owns with Jim Porter a writing service, The Write Brothers. Dobkins lives in Arizona with his wife Marty. They have a son, daughter, seven grandchildren, and two cats that won't go away.

Contents

Contents (cont.)

Contents (cont.)

Introduction

Sometimes evil is so out in the open that it goes unnoticed. Thirty-one years had elapsed from the time Dennis Rader bound, tortured and killed four members of the Otero family on January 15, 1974 until his arrest February 25, 2005. He confessed to ten murders committed over 17 years.

When I asked former Park City policeman Dan Lickey how Rader was able to pull this off, he shook his head. "Plain dumb luck."

Probably no man was hated more by Rader than Lickey, who along with others at City Hall had dismissed Rader as being a weirdo who was not good at socializing with people. Looking back, Lickey's biggest regret is that on one particular occasion he did not recognize Rader's actions for what they really were—the demeanor of a man who was hiding something. This occasion will be revealed later in this book.

I interviewed Lickey and others during a one-week visit to Kansas in November 2006 in which I finally got to meet Mary Capps in person. Her zest for life and the twinkle in her eyes gave no hint of her months-long bout with Post Traumatic Stress Syndrome, which she'd been diag-nosed as having in the wake of her boss' arrest as the BTK serial killer. She appeared as fully recovered as is possible.

Mary's dad, George, former Police Chief of Park City, called Rader a "strange ranger...a lazy ass...a coward."

George Capps said his biggest regret was "not doing more to get City Hall to take action with regard to Mary's complaints about Dennis. I did not want people to think I was favoring Mary because she was my daughter."

His face reddened and his neck veins strained moments after beginning to discuss City Hall's refusal to erase Mary's negative job reviews posted by Rader.

"How would you feel if a serial killer gave you a bad job review...and his supervisor would not even consider expunging it from your employment records AFTER the guy was arrested as a serial killer? It's just not right. She will be a victim of Dennis Rader as long as those job performance reviews remain on file for any prospective employer to check out."

I later told Mary what her dad had said and how strongly he regretted not supporting her cause while she still worked under Rader's supervision, that she would be proud of his defense of her.

George Capps revealed another strong regret, which was that he had endorsed the campaign of the current mayor.

"She used Mary in her bid to become mayor," her dad said, "calling her 'My friend.' Then, once mayor, she did a 180 and opposed Mary. And I helped get her elected. Now I regret supporting her."

While I was in Park City and vicinity, Mary gave me a tour of Dennis' neighborhood. A lasting impression I have is of facing five particular houses. Picture this in your mind—the house to the far right is the house where Rader lived with his wife Paula and their children. Four houses to the far left on the corner is the house, 6254 Independence, in which Rader murdered Marine Hedge in 1985—and in the house right in the middle is where Paula lived with her mother.

"My God," I thought. "How could any woman live two doors down from the house she'd lived in so many years in the presence of the BTK killer and two doors from the house in which he committed one of the murders? In my mind this did not, and still does not compute.

(The house Dennis Rader lived in was demolished on March 7, 2007 as the first step by Park City to create a new entryway to Jardine Memorial Park.)

One question I asked of nearly everyone I talked to in Park City and neighboring communities was, "Do you think Paula knew or suspected her husband was the BTK killer?"

The response I most often got was, "I don't see how she could not have suspected him, especially with all those things he kept in their bedroom closet."

Violet Capps, Mary's mother, had a more direct assessment. "She's either on the moon or in denial about her husband. How could she not know? She had to be curious about what was in that closet."

I asked her, "What would you do if you found out your husband was a serial killer?"

"I'd turn him in in a heartbeat."

George said, "We shouldn't jump to conclusions about Paula. We have no way of knowing what she knew or was thinking."

Violet got up from a chair at the dinette table and walked the several feet onto the back patio of their home to puff a cigarette. That was when George's neck veins began to strain. I said, "I don't want you to have a heart attack."

Violet heard my comment through the open arcadia door, and laughed. "He always does that when he gets worked up about something."

Mary's parents wear well their many years of marriage. He's inches over 6-feet tall and in good physical shape; she's a short wisp of a woman. Kind of a Mutt and Jeff duo. Good people.

In meeting a wide assortment of aunts, uncles, cousins, and siblings, there is one common thread running through Mary's family—no one has a difficult time expressing their opinions. I found this quite refreshing.

We've put this book together secretively, the goal being to announce its existence as close to the actual publication date as possible. We did this to avoid not only premature publicity, but also the prying eyes of those who might not be too happy about the truth this book conveys.

The few people who knew beforehand about my involvement with this project, virtually without exception, asked, "How did you wind up working with Mary?"

It's a fair question. Desiring that her full story be told truthfully, Mary sought out a way to achieve that. She made contact with Ron Watkins, who runs perhaps the most successful book writing service on the Internet. His time availability was severely limited due to other commitments, so he asked me if I would consider taking over the project. He and I have both written or co-authored multiple crime books. He thought it would be a good fit for me. I agreed. Mary, in turn, agreed to working with a new co-author.

How do you recover the loss of six-and-one-half years of your life?

This book, although it does intertwine the evil deeds of Dennis Rader with various time periods of Mary's life, it is not so much about the BTK killer as it is about a woman whose innocent childhood hopes and dreams morphed into terrible nightmares under his work supervision.

The nightmares didn't stop with Rader's arrest on February 25, 2005. They intensified. Literally crippled by stress and fear, months of psychological counseling enabled her to start reclaiming her life, and a gradual return toward being the person she was before her hire to work for Rader.

Having heard her story, I concur that she indeed was the next victim. Being supervisor in the two-person Compliance Dept for the City of Park City was the perfect cover. It afforded the opportunity for Rader to keep his nastiness against Mary secretive and tormenting. There is strong reason to believe that Rader was gradually

poisoning her to affect her enough physically and mentally that she would quit her job. And then he would kill
her, as he suspected she was getting too close to figuring
out that he was the BTK killer.

Jim Dobkins
May 18, 2007

Prologue: A nightmarish moment

It was in May of 2004—just weeks after BTK re-emerged, teasing police detectives with his messages and BTK *Field Grams*—that it happened.

Dennis called me into his office and started berating me about one of the forms that he claimed I had failed to get to him. I told him that I had already turned it in, and he said, "If you had, I would have it."

I replied that he probably misplaced it. His eyes and jaw took on that *How dare you speak to me in that tone or disagree with me* look

I went to my portion of our office and was looking in my file cabinet with my back to the door...that's when I heard it close sharply. I snapped up and turned around to see Dennis standing there in front of the door, blocking my only exit. The look on his face was one that I had never seen before. It was like he was in a trance. I told him in a raised voice, and firmly, to open the door. He didn't reply. I said it again:

"Open the damn door, Dennis!"

He started toward me. That's when I grabbed for the phone to intercom for help. The look on his face was pure evil. I punched numbers blindly. First I tried Jack, but he didn't answer.   Then I punched Carol Jones' extension.

"Carol! Help me! Dennis won't open the door. Send someone. Please!"

Dennis knew I was panicked. He calmly reached over and unlocked the door and opened it. He returned back to his desk. When Jack Whitson, Dennis' supervisor, got back there, Dennis had already taken on the appearance as if nothing had happened.

So here we are—my word against Dennis'—and, of course, they believed him at the time. I wonder if that event ever crossed Jack or Carol's mind after Dennis was revealed as BTK.

It's a horrible flashback for me. It's one of the first things I recalled after he was arrested...and for months I would wake up at night with my mind racing, wondering what his intention on that day was.

I didn't like my mind's answer.

One: An uneasy feeling

As usual, I awoke about 6 a.m. on Friday, February 25th, 2005. As I lay in bed staring at the ceiling, an over-whelming dread blanketed me. It was stifling. My stomach knotted. I could feel my heart pounding as I gasped for breath. Thank God my throat did not constrict as it had so many times recently.

My legs cramped, and I thought, *No way could I work with Dennis today. I can't take his crap. Not today.* I could not shake the feeling lately that when I was in the office it was like I was in the presence of Satan—not Dennis. If anybody asked me to spell "evil" I would have slowly, precisely spelled "D e n n i s   R a d e r"...that's how deeply he'd burrowed into my head.

A chill seized my body. I knew what I had to do.

It was too early yet to call in sick so I absorbed some time by eating my usual breakfast: 2 slices of bacon, 2 scrambled eggs, and 1 piece of toast. I chewed very slowly, deliberately, constantly glancing at the time. When the clock hands showed it was almost 8 o'clock, my work report in time, I called, leaving this message, "I have an ear infection and I am seeing my doctor at 2:00 this afternoon."

I'd made the doctor's appointment minutes before I called in, so I wasn't lying about that. Truth is, I did have an ear infection, just not bad enough to not be able to go in to work. My reason for seeing the doctor was to get a release as a way of convincing everyone that I was sick.

Rod, my fiancé, called my cell phone at 9 a.m., just as he did every workday during his break. He seemed upset that I stayed home from work.

The rest of the morning I piddled around my duplex apartment, finally taking a shower. I'd just stepped out when the phone rang. It was Rod. He asked, "What are you doing?"

"I'm getting ready to go see the doctor. Why are you calling?"

"We got off work early." (He's an assembler at Optima Bus Corporation.)

"In that case," I replied, "pick up a hamburger and drop it off on your way home."

"Okay."

About ten minutes later he called again. "Have you heard what's going on?"

"Why?"

"I'm in the drive-through at Spangles. Dennis' work truck is parked on the side of the road. Cops are everywhere, and a big truck is blocking the road in front of Dennis' house, and crime tape is up."

(You have a clear view of the street in front of Dennis' house from the drive-through at Spangles.)

"Knock it off, Rod. Quit joking around."

"I'm not joking."

I still didn't believe him, so when he arrived at my duplex, he said, "Get in the car."

He drove me down the street while I ate the burger. By this time there were news media everywhere, and Dennis' truck was gone. We listened to the radio and didn't hear anything. I thought that a citizen had had enough of his crap and injured Dennis, so I called into work and asked what was going on. I was told that Jack (mine and Dennis' superior) and the Mayor needed to see me. "Just as soon as I iron my uniform," I said.

I canceled my doctor's appointment. Back at my duplex, while I pressed my uniform, Rod turned on the TV to see if anything was on about what was going on. Whatever it was, it hadn't hit the news.

Arriving at work, I was quickly ushered into counsel chambers where Jack Whitson (Director of Economic Planning and Development) and Mayor Emil Bergquist awaited. I took two steps into the room, suddenly unnerved by the sound of someone else closing the door behind me.

Jack, wearing a Khaki color jacket with large pockets at the hips, button-up plaid shirt, twill slacks, and lace-up brown shoes, sat on the edge of one table. The Mayor, who reminded me of Ned Flanders from *The Simpson's* with his thick unruly hair, I believe, was attired as usual in a button-up-the-front shirt, and faded blue jeans. He always had an unkempt appearance.

Bergquist did the talking. My mouth gaped open at his terse words. "We're complying with a Federal Investigation. You are on paid vacation until further notice."

Gathering myself, I asked, "Am I being investigated?"

"I can't tell you."

"Am I the only City employee being sent home?"

"Yes."

"Well, what am I and the other employees to think?"

This pissed Bergquist off, and he left the room.

Jack said, "You can't go into your office. FBI, KBI, and police officers are in there."

"Can I go to the break room?"

"Yes."

When I turned down the hall to go to the break room, that is when I got a clear view of mine and Dennis's office, and I saw many people, most in suits, and some wearing jackets that were marked on the back FBI or KBI. I started shaking. I left City Hall and went home, and looked in the phone book for an attorney. That's when I found Tad Wagner.

Most of that afternoon I paced my apartment, chain smoking, holding the remote in my hand surfing channels to find out what the hell was going on. My mind went on overdrive. *Are they going to show up and haul me off in cuffs? What could I have done? Who wanted to have me investigated?*

It was mental hell.

That evening the news media started speculating on the BTK—Bind, Torture, Kill—serial killer, but it didn't make sense to me since I was sent home. By 10 p.m. there'd been an announcement that the Wichita Police Department would hold a news conference at 10 a.m. the following morning.

I couldn't sleep that night. My mind would not shut down. It was a great relief that I had company to watch the news conference—my sister Michelle, Rod; and duplex neighbor Cassey.

When Lt. Landwehr stated that Dennis L. Rader had been arrested and charged with the crimes claimed by BTK, I broke down. It was at this time that every conversation that Dennis and I had concerning BTK, as well as the weird things that had occurred at my half of the duplex, the strange calls all in that same month came rushing back, and nothing but fear for what could have happened filled my head.

Jack called right after the conference. "Hide out. The news media are looking for you, because you are a woman and worked for Dennis. Do not talk to anyone."

He didn't ask how I was doing, or say that he was sorry for never listening to me.

Nothing.

I was on my own. I did go into hiding at Rod's house in Wichita, behind a padlocked, six-foot security fence that surrounded his property.

I let Tad deal with Park City.

My cell phone wouldn't quit ringing, so I also changed my number. I thought, *Isn't it amazing that no one wanted to listen to me complain about the son of a bitch when he was just Dennis Rader...but now that he's known as BTK , everyone wants every little juicy detail. Well, I'm not talking.*

And I didn't talk, except when necessary in regard to the lawsuit filed by Tad against Park City. I still get pissed just thinking about the good old boys hunkered down at City Hall. They remind me of ostriches with their heads buried in the sand, hiding in their façade worlds.

Now I'm talking.

In this book.

"Mary will always be a victim of BTK
because he got into her head."

George Capps

Two: Project Broadwater

Two events nearly numbed and traumatized my mind into oblivion: finding out the day after his arrest that my boss was the BTK killer; and learning the depth of his depravity during his sentencing hearing August 17 and 18, 2005.

I say two events, because when it was pointed out to me that I probably was Project Broadwater—Rader's intended 11th murder victim—I already was numbed beyond other people's understanding.

Maybe it was fitting that the hearing was held during the dog days of August, as Rader was called Park City's chief dogcatcher. The weather was brutal outside, the kind of sultry days when you think you can't perspire another ounce—but you do; the sweat saturating your clothes and dampening your spirits. It was hot as hell inside my fiancé's home, where I was staying in seclusion. I remember this because the air conditioning went out. I wore shorts and white T-shirts to keep as cool as possible. The sweat just was unbearable. I took a lot of quick showers to bring down my body temperature. Knowing I'd have to do this, I'd purchased VHS tapes to tape the hearing, and watched as much of it as I could stomach.

But showers, good as they were for keeping my body cool, did little to calm the anger in my soul, the hurt of being ignored. Was there nothing that could do THAT?"

Court TV carried the live feed from Judge Gregory Waller's courtroom inside Sedgwick County Courthouse in Wichita.

I cringed when they showed Rader on camera. My skin began to crawl and anger welled up in me. I was sickened by looking at him as well as trying to forget him. It brought flashbacks to his horrible demeanor that I hated every day for the previous six-and-a-half years.

I remember that the media was talking about his demeanor, and I was thinking, *if they could see it now, why was I the only one that saw it before the public did that I was at his mercy?*

I hated him. I hated the people that ignored me. I felt all alone. I wanted to talk to somebody for hours on end when it hit me to talk even if it was in the middle of the night—not that I wanted a response; I just wanted to talk out loud the rushing thoughts in my head. I believe that those closest to me were frustrated because they understood that I was going through something they couldn't understand but didn't know how to respond. I chain smoked, drank a lot of beer just to try to stay dumb and go to sleep without anxiety and nightmares.

Can you fathom hearing about the pictures of girls he cut out of magazines and newspapers and named them and then rode with them in the city vehicle...only to recall the time in 2001 when you walked up to his truck to see a picture on the seat next to him of a blonde girl in a bra and you try to excuse it in your mind? I told others about this when it happened, and I remember calling him a freak at the time.

There are so many things that made me know that son of a bitch was going to kill me...in my gut I know but without proof people will assume that I'm nuts. That's okay—let them. I only pray that they never find themselves in a position that no one ever believes them. I've felt stuck in that position for years, ever since I filed my first grievance against Dennis Rader while working in the Park City Compliance Department.

After it was released that BTK's last project was Project Broadwater—all his actual and intended victims were called Project this or Project that—my mother told me she had broken his code.

"What are you talking about," I said. She had my very sudden full attention.

"Well, Broad could mean Broadway—you live less than a block off of Broadway. Water could mean a body of water, right? There is that water lagoon directly behind the duplex you live in. The way that rat makes up code names for everything and everybody…"

"Holy shit!" I exploded. "I hadn't thought about that."

"And don't forget what he said about the construction on the streets…"

There was construction, trenching going on Broadway and on my street—that, coupled with a series of frightening things that happened during the weeks leading up to Rader's arrest—kept Rader from carrying out his plan for me, which was described in terrifying detail on the second day of the hearing.

First, though, here is what was reported on page 56 of the document THE STATE OF KANSAS vs. DENNIS L. RADER:

An intended eleventh victim was identified (during the 32 hours Rader was questioned on February 25 and 26 after his arrest). "Project Broadwater or Broadwater, I tried to hit on her the day I dropped the Number Two off at the UPS box. It was a run, it was a go and everything, but they were working on the roads…They were working on the curbs. One of those things you don't foresee…So what in the hell do you do? You just do a back up and wait for another day. I was going to try it in the spring or fall." The intended eleventh victim was selected as "a target, because she had a routine. People that have routines are trouble with me.

"That's what I am always looking for is routines."

Rader knew exactly what my schedule was at all times, when I'd take a sick day, whatever. Sick days happened more often toward the end, during the months I believe Rader was gradually poisoning me in an effort to get me to quit my job so it would make it easier for him to kill me. I'll tell you about that later in this book. It gives me the shivers just thinking about it. He stormed in anger after I finally could not take it any more and had announced I was quitting, only to let his supervisor, Jack Whitson, talk me out of it.

Looking back, I believe he would have killed me in a heartbeat at the first opportunity.

My stomach curdled and my breath came in sharp gasps during Lt. Ken Landwehr's testimony during the second day of the hearing when he discussed Project Broadwater. It was one of many hearing moments in which comments kept echoing in my head—one of those moments I wish I could bend over, turn my head sideways and shake the thoughts out forever.

Lt Landwehr related a conversation with Rader in which BTK said victim number eleven was going to be wrapped entirely in plastic and, of course, strangled. He would bind her ankles, her neck and everything. He would put I-bolts in the ceiling, and use pulleys to hoist up and stretch the body out—put it up there so that when the police officers entered they'd see the body on display.

The items needed to carry out this plan were found stashed in Rader's home.

I felt like vomiting.

One of the hearing's many disgusting revelations was that early in his teen years, Dennis already had a fetish for wearing women's clothes and under-garments. I was rendered almost speechless—and that's hard to do—when the prosecution displayed a self-taken photo of him hanging in the basement of his parents' home decked out in women's clothes. Even though the photo was not shown to viewers in Kansas, my brain captured the image. Too bad the rope didn't cut off his oxygen long enough to end the sicko's life right then and there.

Three: The dreams girls dream

My mother, Violet Maxine Capps, gave birth to me on February 2, 1960 in Wichita, about a few months after Dennis Rader took those self-photos of himself in dangerous bondage situations. I'm the oldest of the five children that she and my father, George Felix Capps, ushered into this world. Sister Michelle followed on July 31, 1961; brothers Hobert on November 5, 1963, and Jeffery on February 23, 1970; and sister Kimberly on March 5, 1973.

My early years were normal with teddy bears and bunnies attending the tea parties my sister Michelle and I would stage when we were little girls. But nothing prepared me for the horrors of facing Dennis Rader. As you will see.

At first I could not believe my former boss had been doing such weird stuff since before I was even born, but then as horrible deed after horrible deed was revealed to millions of viewers around the world, I told myself, *Yeah, you could, you perverted monster.*

My childhood was mirrored in network television shows that unapologetically depicted families with traditional values. As the oldest, I learned early on that I had to take responsibility for my actions. Yet with the births of my brothers and sisters spread over thirteen years, I never lost the feeling of being loved equally by my father and mother. It gave me balance, allowing me freedom to dream the dreams that girls dream in rural Kansas. I'd lay on my back on the cool grass and look up at the sky, and watch the clouds as they lazily transformed into animals and other things. Other times I'd just lay there, eyes closed, willing my mind to revel in the possibilities of life—falling in love, followed by a magical wedding day then having children.

I flourished as a child at a time when children were allowed, well, to be children. It didn't matter if it was winter or summer, we were outdoors, not planted in front of video games. No, back then, entertainment was playing outdoors with the other neighborhood children, waiting for the ice cream truck in the summer, playing "Mother, may I?" and "Red Light Green Light."

Staying outdoors for hours and hours was the norm. It was expected. And it was safe. We explored the neighborhood, riding our bikes, with playing cards attached to the spokes with clothes pins; the sound of many playing cards on bicycles could be heard in the houses when we'd see who could attach the most cards, and then race up and down the street.

The fun would abruptly end when our mothers could be heard yelling out the front doors to come home for dinner. It's a sound you don't hear anymore, the sound of loving mothers calling their brood home. Sadly, it would become a forgotten noise drowned out in later years by cell phones. Another sound I would grow to miss is the sound of a wooden screen door slamming shut while my friends and I were running out the door to catch up with the other children for the daily adventure.

But all good summers had to end. The sound of the locust signaled that school was about to start up again, and the lazy days of summer would soon be over.

My grandmother—Dad's mother—used to always call me on my birthday and ask me how her "Groundhog" was doing. I miss that. She passed away in November 1987. Grandma and Grandpa had celebrated their 50th wedding anniversary just two months earlier, and there was a big celebration; there was even a band. Grandpa loved to dance so there they were twirling around the dance floor, and then next thing I knew Grandma was gone, and only in her sixties.

I know that my parents struggled sometimes with raising us kids. I don't mean that we were problem children, not any more than any other normal children; just that there were plenty of times they felt the financial strain of five children.

My memories are so classic to the way Hollywood portrayed the '60s and '70s. I know there's no going back, but those memories still give me smiles at times I really need a smile.

We moved to Park City in time for me to start kindergarten at Chisholm Trail Elementary. Mom and Dad preached, "Don't take candy from a stranger...don't get in the car with a stranger." Mom took me to school every day, and picked me up. It's what moms did to protect their children.

One time Mom was late getting to the school. I wasn't scared. I felt grown up now that I was in school, and started the seven-block walk toward home, north on West Parkview. A neighbor lady drove up and asked if I needed a ride home. "No," I proudly said, "I'm not supposed to take rides from strangers." Well, the neighbor lady and my parents were tickled by this.

When I was in the third grade I was a "Brownie" (Girl Scouts). In order for my sister Michelle and me to get our cooking badge we had to prepare a meal. So we cooked scrambled eggs, toast, and bacon. Mom about gagged; the house was filled with smoke and everything was over done. Mom's sister (Aunt Bernice) came over that morning, and bless her heart, she made Michelle and I feel like we were ready for gourmet cooking.

My family reflected the mores still typical in the country's heartland in the '60s and '70s. When I and my siblings went someplace Dad told us to be quiet until spoken to. We knew what that meant—don't run around making all kinds of noise, and acting like a pack of wild heathens. Our parents were complimented for the positive public image their children portrayed. When we addressed an aunt or uncle we were not allowed to call them by just their first name; we had to address them with proper protocol. Everybody knew Grandpa—Dad's father—by *Pappy*, including our cousins, but not us—it was *Grandpa*.

You know, our parents showered us with love and still do, but they could never be accused of spoiling us. I love my parents; they are two of the finest people I know. I can't imagine ever losing either of them, because at times they are my strength, and so are my siblings, as well as my extended family.

Michele and I, for some reason I don't think either of us can explain, have always bickered, and still do. We can be in the middle of a heated argument, and the next minute planning our Saturday afternoon together. We were very close, then and now, and are still each other's confidante. When we were little we'd lay at opposite ends of the bed and leg wrestle until Mom or Dad heard us and came in yelling that they didn't want to hear another peep, telling us to get into own beds. As our parent would leave the room, both us of would whisper, "peep."

In the middle of my eighth grade year, Dad was promoted to a supervisor's position for a trucking firm, and our family relocated to Potwin, a farming community with a population of about 500. I went to school in Elbing, Kansas, all the way through my junior year at Remington High School.

Living in that rural farm setting was just plain fun, and the things I and my friends did often also were just plain stupid. We'd go riding around at night on country roads and drive fast and turn out the headlights as we listened to FogHat play Slow Ride. There was no bowling alley, no movie theater in Potwin; nothing, so we had to invent things to do. The store and local business shut down at 6 p.m. You knew it was 6 p.m. because a whistle blew.

About 260 students attended Remington High School. I thought it was really neat that most of the kids were already driving.

I'd taken a condensed Driver's Ed course during the summer between 8th and 9th grades. I started driving at 14 and had my first car—a 1963 Chevy Impala—at 15. But that didn't last long. I thought the only thing that powered the car was a soda in my hand and two bucks of gas. When the car threw a rod for lack of oil Dad was not a happy camper.

That rod was not the only thing that was going bad about the same time.

The year before, on January 15, 1974—eighteen days before my 14th birthday—a 28-year-old man began his descent into infamy. The world would finally learn his identity 31 years later on February 26, 2005—one day after his arrest.

"It started in grade school. I used to make sketches even back then. Annette Funicello was my favorite fantasy hit target when she was on the Mouseketeers. She was a dream girl for a lot of guys. I had these imaginary stories of how I was going to get her, kidnap her, and do sexual things to her in California."

BTK

Four: Evil descends

I chose to let the self-admitted "Monster" document his depravity in his own words. The revelations were revealed to BTK Task Force officers during thirty-two plus hours of questioning after his arrest. I've interwoven his confessions with my narrative so you will know what was going on in my life at the same time. For me, this was a painful process, but I think it will help you and other readers better understand the trauma I went through under Dennis Rader's supervision and afterward.

He is a remorseless man who loved to kill. He got sexually aroused watching his victims die a slow, brutally agonizing death. And he loved baiting and taunting law enforcement officers.

You can sense the evil as he relishes telling how he stalked then slaughtered four members of the Otero family during the daytime on January 15, 1974.

Joseph Otero, Sr., 38
Julie Otero, 34
Josephine Otero, 11
Joseph (Joey) Otero, Jr., 9

This is what he said:

I am totally a lone wolf. Bondage is my forte. If I have sex, I would rather have the bondage. You know, I could still perform with my wife and everything, but that's the way I like to have sex. Because I like to have that person under control.

I always walked the Twin Lakes Mall with the—my hit kit, my gun or the stuff in my car. And just basically, as you call it, trolling. I started trolling other areas of town. I took my wife to work one day, and—she worked at the VA—she didn't like to drive in the ice and snow, so I'm sure that's what it was, I took her one day. When I was on my way home, either in the red car or the Chevette, I saw the Oteros...I saw her and the kids...Yeah, I think they were backing out. I think they were backing out of the driveway

I thought this might work. So—and I've always had kind of a—I've always liked Hispanic people, the dark eyes and dark hair. And I guess they just turn me on. So my main intention was to get her...Mrs. Otero and the girl. I stalked them maybe two or three weeks. [When I entered the Otero home] I didn't know he [Mr. Otero] was home and I didn't—I didn't know about the boy.

I've always had a sexual desire for younger women so I thought Josephine would be my primary target... Project Little-Mex...My original idea was to get Mrs. Otero and Josephine in bed and have sex with them and strangle them. But I didn't really have a good control of the family...they were freaking out and stuff.

[Joey] let the dog out and I came in and I confronted the family. Mr. Otero said, "Is this a joke or something?" He said, "My brother-in-law put you up to this."

I said, "No, this is not a joke. I have a weapon, a .22 with the hollow points I would use."

So they started to lay down in the living room [like I told them].   I bound them as best I could...think I used adhesive tape. I already had my cords with me, and I think some of them were already tied, I mean pre-knotted. I tied Mr. Otero first. Mainly I wanted to restrict him. And I tied Mrs. Otero next.

[The Oteros were now in the master bedroom.]

I used a russ [ruse]. I just told them I was going to California; I needed money, and I needed—I needed a car.   And I was going—oh, I used that on several people—I said I needed food—kind of persuasion and controlling. You get—you win—if people think they are going to be okay, yeah, they are going to be out of harm's way, basically there's going to be a minimum and you got them.

They started complaining about their hands and circulation problems. I thought Mrs. Otero was pretty comfortable, although she was tied. She was on the bed. Mr. Otero and little Joseph were on the floor. Josephine was by her mom.

Decision time...they were going down.

I think I started with him [Mr. Otero] then all hell broke loose when they found out I was going after them. I got him down, put the bag over his head...and he went ballistic, trying to chew a hole in it. And he was still...moving around. So I put the coup de grace [sic] on him. I put either a T-shirt or a plastic bag over his head and latched that thing down tight. I don't think I strangled him yet. I figured that would do it.

I strangled Mrs. Otero and she passed out.

I put a bag over [Joey] Joseph, and then—and then she [Mrs. Otero] yelled at me, that "You killed my boy! You killed my boy!" And she was just going ballistic...that's when I strangled her again and put a pillow over her head, over her face. Josephine, she was crying, "What did you do to my momma? Momma! Momma! Momma!" And in the interim, I had already strangled Josephine, and she came back. You strangle a person and you don't hold them long enough, they will come back. I—I didn't know that. I never strangled a person before. You know I strangled dogs and cats, but I never strangled a person before, so those were the first...strangling is a hard way to kill a person, you know, they don't go down in a minute like they do in the movies. But basically a person passes out. I didn't know they would come back. I figured once you strangled a person, they would be done for. But you don't keep that air—if that air gets back in, although it's probably damaged, if you can breathe, the air is going to come back, and you're going to come back. And that's—basically that was part of my—that's actually my—the BTK, the torture, that's actually my torture is the psychological. You know you're being strangled, that's your torture.

I took him [Joey] to the other room, and put a T-shirt over his head and [then] a plastic bag. I put the T-shirt over the head so they couldn't breathe through it [plastic bag]—so they couldn't chew through it. I leaned from [what happened with] Mr. Otero. I set the chair to watch. I think I put him [Joey] on the bed and I think he rolled off and he was expired there.

I remember problems with Josephine because her hair was in the way...I strangled her, she went out. She was crying, "Momma, Momma," and then somewhere along the line, she woke back up. So my encore was to just take her down there and hang her. If she had been dead, I would have still hung her, just to hang her....her, and then probably masturbate or whatever.

I took her down in the basement, pulled her pants down, and I pulled her top up. I maybe cut her bra. I think I did that after I strangled her. I tied her up a little bit more, tied her ankles, and tied her knees; she already had her hands behind her back—and found the sewer pipe.

And she says, "What's going to happen to me?"

I said, "Well, honey, you're going to be in heaven tomorrow with the rest of your family."

I used to do bondage in basements. At the folks' [his parents] home when they weren't around. It's symbolic, like a dungeon, dark...the best place to hang somebody, solid. It's the same kind of sewer pipe that's in my folks' house, same kind of design and everything.

I already had the rope laid on...just grabbed it and pulled her up. When she was dying, I grabbed my handkerchief out and went off. So I pulled my dick out, my penis out. I don't think I pulled my pants down. It went fast. [The semen] went on the floor. I saw it...It was a big, big wad...right there by Josephine...nobody knew about the DNA then. I thought if I ever had to be put away I wanted to be hung. But I guess they don't do that anymore.

It still makes me cry, the mental image of Dennis hanging Josephine so her toes were only a fraction of an inch off the floor, just so he could increase the suffering and terror. What a deranged mind—getting his jollies off, watching an 11-year-old girl struggle for each breath.

Three members of the Otero family were in school that morning: Charlie, 15; Danny, 14; and their sister, Carmine, 13. Josephine and Joey were about to leave for school when Dennis showed up at their home.

In the STATE OF KANSAS vs. DENNIS L. RADER document filing, it was reported that Dennis feared Charlie. "Yes, especially the one out in New Mexico. He's going to cut me up and feed me to the sharks ...Well, hopefully he won't find me."

It tore me apart as despicable revelation after revelation was intoned by witnesses and prosecuting attorneys. Everyone in the gallery seats was silent. It was so hushed in the courtroom that if anyone had dropped a pin, it would have sounded like a cannon shot.

You will read later about how the daydreams of my childhood morphed into nightmares that terrorized me even months before my boss was discovered to be the BTK serial killer. My psychologist told me it was my subconscious warning me of danger.

Closer and closer to the time of his arrest, the feeling of evil surrounding him grew more intense. I just hadn't picked up all the signs that pointed to my boss. Maybe I had just heard it said way too many times: "He's just being Dennis."

I believe that every pretty girl that Dennis came in contact with was a fantasy for him, from the girl that cut his hair to the girl that checked him out at the store. It was just a matter of what was going to give him the most pleasure from dominance.

Five: A brief lull

You know, while we were living in Potwin, and I was going to Remington High School, things that Dennis did just didn't touch us. We were in a safe community. What I mean to say by this is that Wichita had its crime—well, listening to it on the news was like listening to something that was happening in New York.

We were S A F E!

The most that I felt affected was that I wasn't dating or going out anywhere at night except with my parents.

There was talk by some adults, likening the Otero murders to the Clutter family—father, Herb; mother, Bonnie; son, Kenyon; and daughter, Nancy. The Clutters were murdered on Saturday, November 15, 1959 in a farmhouse near Holcomb and Garden City, in west central Kansas. Truman Capote wrote about the murders as a "novelized" true story in his book, *In Cold Blood*.

People who didn't lock their doors, started locking them for awhile—until they got comfortable, and then went back to leaving them unlocked.

Aside from that, our respective routines hardly skipped a beat. Mom still told me to keep my head and ears covered in the winter cold when I left each weekday morning to catch the school bus. Michelle and I still bickered with one another one minute and were best buds again the next minute. I still daydreamed, only now, instead of seeing animals, those images were replaced by cars and more grown-up things. I enjoyed looking for that silver lining that really wasn't behind every cloud. That didn't bother me—I knew a silver lining was behind every cloud I looked at—it just was invisible at times.

If I wanted to know what time the sun would rise or set the next day, there was always a *Farmer's Almanac* close by. Everything about my world seemed in order. I knew my life was going to be one of never-ending good things happening to me. My daydreams would all come true. I knew I'd live happily ever after—just like in those stories I loved to hear as a little girl.

Then the news erupted with reports of Kathryn Bright's murder on April 4, 1974—only 79 days after the Otero murders. This shook up some of the residents of Potwin. People who'd still never locked their doors began locking them.

My daydreams began to be less positive, less reassuring. Sure, I still daydreamed now and then, sometimes leaning my head back from a car's back seat so I could look up at the stars through the rear window. But the murderer, who would later that year introduce himself to the world as BTK, had crept—if only slightly—into my distant thoughts.

And I wondered, "He wouldn't come to Potwin, would he?"

Dennis had codes for everything. For example, SBT stood for "Sparky Big Time"—meaning an erection. AFLV was short for "After Life Concept of Victim." Here are BTK's comments about his "AFLV" plans for the Otero family:

"Joseph Otero will be a bodyguard in the afterlife. Julie will bathe me and be my female servant in the bathroom area. Joseph II will be a boy servant and male sex toy at times. Josephine will be my star young maiden that I will teach sex to..."

Six: The "Dumb Luck" Monster

You could not guess how many times I've wanted to turn back the clock—anything so Dennis Rader wound never have existed. He nearly destroyed my life, literally and physically. Yet what I went through does not begin to compare with the terror the victims themselves and their survivors went through.

Someone asked me if I felt a bond with his victims. I would honestly have to say that I do not—never have. I do, however, feel a bond with the survivors of the victims. Like they did, I felt as if no one could possibly feel as I did.

How can you make others understand in words what it's like to see or experience evil—pure evil?

Sure, we all know evil is real . . . but to have it touch your life in a such a profound manner that you cannot conceive how you will ever be normal again . . . *that* gnaws away at you, steals your self-esteem, and you always keep asking yourself, "Why can't others see this and understand my pain?"

I know that Kevin Bright did.

As I saw Kevin sitting in the gallery during the sentencing hearing and heard the testimony of the horrors he and his sister, Kathryn Bright, went through, I saw the pain lingering in his face, his eyes.

I knew he'd asked himself the same question.

Kevin was 19, five-feet-six inches tall and weighed 116 pounds when he broke his bindings and fought for his and his sister's life. I mention his size, because in Dennis' confession he recalled Kevin as a "big guy." Kevin did have a big heart. I believe he still does.

Kathryn Bright was 21 when BTK took her life.

These are Dennis's own words about Kathryn and Kevin.

Sweet kid. So what do you want to know? She was Project Lights Out.

Basically . . . out trolling . . . I spotted her one day going in the house with one of her friends. And she fit that profile . . . the BTK profile. The trolling stage moved to the stalking stage . . . used squeeze ball to develop strength to strangle someone. You can't strangle a person very easy; it's a hard business. Your hands go numb after a while unless you have your hands in shape . . . it might take two or three minutes. You got to put pressure, you know, wrap it around their necks.

I want to get to the person in the house. You drive by the house, you walk around the house. In fact, I went there a couple of times and knocked just to see if she was home.

[And he said this about the day he killed her:]

I had stuff ready to go but she wasn't home . . . she was picked out. I just saw her go in the house one day. I thought, *Well, this might work.* I didn't have any idea she had a brother.

This was locked in on that day . . . I said, "This is the day."

My plan was to pose as a WSU student. I had my school books, went up to the porch. I knocked on the front door, and no one answered. I thought, *Oh gee, they are not home.* Maybe this is better yet, maybe I can break in. I walked around, low and behold, the screen door was locked. So I just punched it in real quick like. I broke it out...went in. Didn't cut the phone line like I did at the Otero home...changed my MO to throw off the police.

[He broke glass in the process of getting into the house.]

And I thought that was dumb, breaking in that way, because if she comes in the back door, she's going to run, she's not even going to come in the house—a smart person wouldn't. So I swept the glass up. And about the time I got the glass all swept up, I was starting to case the place. Well, they [came] to the front door.

I tried to ease them. I told them I was wanted in California; they had wanted posters out for me. I need a car; I need some food and some money.

I forced them into the bedroom, that's where I—I had her—I had him, I think, tie her up, and then I tied him up [to bedpost in the other bedroom].

Well, naturally, I was going to have to get him out of the way before I did anything to Kathryn. I started strangling him . . . his hands were behind his back. I got the lariat around his neck and it snapped. I didn't have the strong cords . . . I didn't tie his feet tight enough. He broke loose and yanked his feet out and stood up. And I just did one of those John Wayne things.

I'm sorry—this is a human being.

But I am a monster.

I just pop shot, just quick. Just like that. He went down. I thought, *Well, I got him. I shot him,* and I thought, *Oh gee.* Then I went back to her. She heard the gun and she said, "What's going on?"

I said, "Oh, I fired at your brother; I wounded him. He's going to be all right."

She was starting to become hysterical, and going crazy.

Oh, before I did all this, I turned the stereo on. Before I started to strangle him, I turned the stereo up. I thought the sound would distort the strangling sounds or the gagging sounds or whatever. But I wanted him out of the way so I could have my time with her.

He came loose on me [again after being shot in the head]. When we fought again—and he about killed me then, because he got. . .he got his finger on my Magnum. Jeez, I'm going to die right here, you know. He probably saw my Magnum underneath my coat, and he grabbed for that, and put his finger in the trigger. I thought *This sucker is going to go right off . . . It's going to go right off at my chest, and I'm dead.* And so I slipped my finger into the finger guard so he couldn't pull the trigger. Anyway, we struggled . . . I pulled away and shot him with the .22, and he went down again.

[Actually, that's when] Kathryn heard the gunshots. That's when I went back in there. She started getting all hysterical and going crazy. And I think that's when we started fighting, because just not—I just did not have control over her at all. She couldn't defend herself real good, but she fought like a hell cat.

I tried to strangle her. That didn't work. I was losing control. There was no way that I was ever going to do what I wanted to do, and I had to put her down. I just went ahead and drew the knives and slashed her. It was in the back. And then I may have spun her, and stuck her in the front.

I read . . . one of the other killers . . .It's where he would stab his people, stab them right back here under the ribs . . . they were upward thrusts.

She was moaning and groaning. I had blood on my hands, and my pants, and my feet; what a mess. I didn't realize human blood was so slick, very slick. I had it on the shoes. You probably found footprints, I don't know. But I was a mess. I had some kind of suede shoes. I know I got blood on them. I know I got Kathleen's blood all over them after I stabbed her.

I had no intent of either shooting a person or stabbing them . . . that wasn't my forte, but that just happened because I lost control of it and I had to do something quick. They are all sexual overt. They are either going to be bound and strangled or suffocated or hung, or something, one of those three. The only reason I knifed

Kathleen was because I was losing control, and I had to get out of there.

I heard the door open, and I said, "Oh shit." The police are coming in; I'm going to be dead meat.

[Actually, Kevin had gotten up and had run out the door.]

". . . saw him streaking across the—you know, streaking across town going east—westbound. I made fast tracks out of there. [Kathryn was] moaning and groaning, blood running out of her. I thought, *Should I shoot her?* He [Kevin] had already seen me, didn't make any difference, you know. If he's going to I.D. me, he's going to I.D. me. It won't make any difference with her, so I don't need to shoot her. And I didn't have time to strangle her. So I basically booked out . . . ran all the way back up. I almost went all the way to the main campus, because that's where I parked my car. That was a long run. I figured, yeah, the police are going to be coming down this street at any time and I'm in deep doo-doo

I went home and cleaned it [the knife he used to stab Kathryn. He sometimes referred to her as Kathryn, other times as Kathleen], immaculate cleaned . . . I washed it and washed it and washed it and washed it, because I knew if they ever got me and they found that with her blood in there, I was cooked.

I got home before my wife got home. I planned to burn my clothes but I couldn't burn them at that time; I had a time frame to work under. I had to get back and get cleaned up because Paula was going to be home, my wife . . . I had my gun and some of my stuff over there at my folks' house. Dad had an old saw box with sawdust . . . I put my gun in there.

My AFLV for Kathleen? She was to be a bondage girl. [In his world of "codes" AFLV meant "After Life

Concept of Victim"—he envisioned an "afterlife" assignment for each of his victims.]

Normally I'm a pretty nice guy. I'm sorry, but I am.
You know, I've—you know, I've raised kids, I had a wife,
and, you know, president of the church, been in Scouts.
It goes on and on. But, yeah, I have a mean streak in
me, so . . . and it occasionally flares up, takes control.

Kathryn lived for several more hours, dying on a surgery
table. And, although Kevin gave an accurate description
of Dennis, he went unnoticed by the police. I think former
policeman Dan Lickey's comment on why Dennis went
unsuspected and uncaught all those years is right on
target:

"Just plain dumb luck."

Dad, awakened from a deep sleep, had stormed outside to find out what all the commotion was about. In no uncertain terms he informed Allen, "As a boy growing up on a ranch, honking the horn is how we called the cattle in to feed, not how by God you're going to visit my daughter! Park the car and knock on the door!"

Seven: My glory years

There were maybe 500 people living in Potwin vs. probably 600 to 700 times that many living in Wichita—the Big City. I'm talking BIG difference. Although we were only about 45 minutes to the northwest of Wichita, we were in another world. It was a world where folks still stopped to smell the roses. Seven to eight hours' nightly sleep was the norm rather than the exception. Most folks went to bed early, got up early, worked hard, and did things on the weekends with their families.

Sure, everybody knew everybody else, but that wasn't necessarily a bad thing. You always knew there was a helping hand if you ever needed one. In that sense, it was like an extended family.

I miss that, even though I don't miss living in a town with no theater, and that virtually closed up at 6 p.m. But at that time in my life, for me, it was a place of comfort. As I told you earlier, the one word that best described Potwin was S A F E. To tell you the truth, the murders happening in Wichita really didn't compute all that much. That was THERE, and I was HERE. Some thoughts nagged at me briefly, but I pushed them aside—life was just too much fun; even my parents' desires that I not go out anywhere at night soon faded; however, they did remind me not to plan any dates or trips that included Wichita. Their safety zone did not extend that far.

The three years I went to high school over in Remington, well, those were my glory years. There were only 268 students my junior year, and that included freshmen, sophomores, juniors, and seniors.

High school was great! Everybody went to the basketball and football games on Friday nights, and during Homecoming everybody dressed up in formals for the dance. The girls would spend weeks getting ready . . . what dress to wear . . . how to wear our hair . . . this lipstick or that lipstick . . . then the excitement of getting a wrist corsage that matched our dress from our dates.

School attire was basic—we always wore jeans and shirts.

On dates, we usually went to see a movie in El Dorado or Newton, Kansas, and had pizza for dinner. During the summer, my best friend, Rosemary Shinn, and I along with my sister, Michelle, would go to El Dorado to cruise the main drag there.

When I was 13, I saw a movie called *Jeremiah Johnson* starring Robert Redford. I fell in love; his eyes just drew me in.

I remember my first date I ever had. It was with Allen Smith. He was a year older than I, a sophomore while I was a freshman. It all started one day on the bus to school two weeks after my freshman year started. My friends Kathy and Karen knew Allen, and told me that he liked me and was wondering if he could sit with me on the bus. I thought about two seconds.

"Yes."

About a week later, he walked me home from the bus stop and gave me a stuffed teddy bear. Then he quit riding the bus because of football practice, but he always said "Hi" to me at school when I arrived and held my hand. Allen was tall, so during the winter he played basketball for Remington. I always went to his home games.

But my first date was football homecoming. My mother made my dress, and it was wonderful. It was long and full in a pretty shade of mint green which, of course, matched my blonde hair and green eyes. Allen gave me a pretty white and light green corsage for my wrist made of carnations.

I felt so grown up at the school dance, dancing away the evening to the theme for Homecoming, *Lady* by Styx. I got my first kiss that night. Allen's older brother drove us home. Then Allen walked me to the door and gave me a kiss goodnight.

After basketball season was over, Allen and I sorta drifted apart but remained good friends. The following year—my sophomore year—Allen got a new car and drove by my house to show it to me. Dad, a strapping six-feet-three, was at home asleep. Us kids were in the car with Mom, and we got there just in time for the fireworks. Well, here my mother is driving up the road, and we see the car parked in the middle of the road in front of our house . . . and my dad stomping out to the car, leaning forward so he could see the person inside as he pointed his finger at Allen. In his excitement to show me his car, he just pulled up in front and started honking the horn. Dad, awakened from a deep sleep, had stormed outside to find out what all the commotion was about. In no uncertain terms he informed Allen, "As a boy growing up on a ranch, honking the horn is how we called the cattle in to feed, not how by God you're going to visit my daughter! Park the car and knock on the door!"

Although I had strawberry blonde hair and green eyes, I was not a bouncy blonde or cheerleader type. But I always had a boyfriend, and was never without a date. I was always invited to the homecoming dances, as well as the proms.

Proms were for juniors and seniors; however, my freshman year I was invited to the prom by one of the most popular guys in school, Mike Eilert, a senior.

My sophomore year I went to prom at Circle High with Richard Sisson. He was my boyfriend at the time, and attended Circle High School in Towanda, which was about 13 miles from where I lived. He rode a motorcycle and I went to a track meet with him, and on our way home we had a wreck. We were both wearing helmets. After that he got a car. That summer he left for wheat harvest—he was saving for college, and wanted to be a doctor. I heard from him in 2001, after all those years. Yes, he had become a doctor and was just touching base with old friends.

I was always trying to do what the boys did, so my freshman year, along with Rosemary and Marsha Cockran, we took shop instead of home ec. Because of that, Grandpa Capps called me Rosie the Riveter. Anyway, we were going to learn to tune up lawnmowers, welding and woodworking. Jimmy Cross, my shop partner, still to this day gives me crap about the time we worked on our lawnmower and he asked for a Phillips screwdriver, to which I replied I didn't know what that was. He says it was my way of keeping from doing the work and getting dirty.

When I was married to my first husband, Russ, I got bored and decided to take some vo tech classes at McPherson College, but the only thing starting that night was welding, so I signed up for the six-week course and passed. End of welding career.

I took home ec my sophomore year and hated it. Rosemary and I kept getting in trouble for not bringing in our sewing assignments, so we would be assigned to cleaning the ovens in class. We preferred that to sewing. Funny thing is I now love to sew.

So you can see, I was an all-American girl, happy, normal and well-adjusted. And you can see I was totally unprepared for the hell that Dennis Rader would put me through as my supervisor, and, later, though I didn't know it, apparently was the man who was planning my death.

"Those three dude [sic] you have in custody are just talking to get publicity for the Otero murders. They know nothing at all. I did it all by myself and with no one's help."

BTK

Eight: "I did it..."

Although Dennis was not very responsible at times when he was my supervisor in the Compliance Department, he for damn sure did not want anybody else taking credit for his murders. I can imagine how angry he became when news broke that three men had been arrested as prime suspects in the Otero murders.

All I remember is that it happened during football season, and I thought, *Some guy wants to take credit for killing four people.* What a jerk. Looking back, I was dead on in calling him a jerk. That's just another four letter work for Dennis Rader.

On October 22, 1974—just two-and-a-half months before my 15th birthday—an unidentified male phoned Don Granger of the *Wichita Eagle* and *Beacon Newspaper*. The man told Granger that a message about the Otero murders was in a book in the Wichita Public Library.

Granger alerted the Wichita Police Department.

Detective Bernie Drowatzky recovered a two-page typed document hidden in a textbook:

Applied Engineering Mechanics.

Law enforcement had arrested three men for the Otero murders.

In the document, the writer said:

"Those three dude [sic] you have in custody are just talking to get publicity for the Otero murders. They know nothing at all. I did it all by myself and with no one's help."

He said, "Let's put it straight", and gave a detailed description of the murders that only the actual killer and the investigating police officers would know. After talking about "the kids making lunches [for school]" and Josephine "hanging by the neck" and Joseph, Jr. being suffocated with the "old bag trick," he added, "Otero's watch missing. I needed one so I took it. Runs good."

The writer claimed that a *Monster* controlled him, and warned that more victims would follow. He said, "The code words for me will be . . . bind them, torture them, kill them . . .

. . . B.T.K."

It would be just two-and-a-half years before the monster would kill again.

During the 32-plus hours of interviewing by various detectives, Dennis explained that he never stops thinking of bondage and could use even the most innocuous item or picture to fantasize.

"Well, there was a cup with a girl on it. You know, I can pick that up and visualize how she would be tied up or something with a gag in her mouth or something. Not a normal person could do that. That's what I did with the slick ads, the slick and models, you know. I would visualize how they would be in my fantasy Death to Pretty Girl Room or torture room, you know, and it's— that's fantasy."

Nine: Happy days

A TV series about a family in Wisconsin frolicked into homes across the nation in 1974. And, like people all over the country, many of the people of Potwin took an almost instant liking to the family of Richie Cunningham. The boys liked his feisty sister Joanie. The girls thought Richie was cute. Both boys and girls loved Arthur "Fonzie" Fonzarelli the *Fonz*—the black-leather-jacketed stud who had a heart-of-gold safe-guarded by his tough-guy reputation.

Happy Days would enjoy a ten-year run. For me, in 1974, the show simply had borrowed use of the definition of what my high school years were—happy days.

I belonged to Kayettes my freshman, sophomore, and junior years. The summer between my sophomore and junior years I attended Kayette summer camp up by Fort Riley, Kansas. My junior year I was President of our school's Kayettes club.

I didn't have a favorite teacher, but the Principal, Mr. Peterson, sticks out in my mind because whenever Rosemary and I got in trouble for being late to class, we would take the swats versus staying after school for detention because we rode the bus. Mr. Peterson gave the swats; however, he was a really good principal.

But I don't want you to get the impression that I was always in trouble—I wasn't, although I did have my moments, just like most of the students did.

Rosemary was a rebel, and I loved her attitude. I remember one time we were walking down the hall when Chuck Sommers made a rude comment to Rosemary. Her reply was to ball her fist and lay him out on the floor. A very attractive girl with long strawberry hair, she had older brothers and had learned how to fight for her position in their pecking order.

She was just plain fun to be with. If you saw Rose-mary, you saw me, and vice-versa.

Through high school my favorite bands and singers were the Rolling Stones, the Eagles, Paul McCartney and Wings, and Elton John. My favorite songs were the ones I remembered through the summers. In 1975, it was *One of these Nights* by the Eagles. My 1976 favorite was *Silly Little Love Sons* by McCartney and Wings, but by 1978, I was listening to Bruce Springsteen.

I dated Bruce Beem the summer between my fresh-man and sophomore year. He had graduated that year, so was already out of school before starting college. Rosemary hated him, but the next summer, between my sophomore and junior year, Rosemary, Michelle and I wanted to go see Heart in concert but it was in Wichita, and Mom and Dad said, "Hell no!"

We asked if we took Bruce could we go. They relented under those conditions. So we asked Bruce, but us three girls had to pool our money that we earned working as waitresses at the Howard Johnson's on the turnpike (Towanada rest area; we worked there for the summer), and we bought Bruce a ticket so that he would go, and we would have a chaperone. I drove one of my parents' cars. It was a 1966 Chevy Nova station wagon with a three-on-the-tree. We drove it when we were out cruising that summer and also raced it, and to our pleasure, did fairly well.

One night Rosemary, Michelle and I wanted to hang out in El Dorado to cruise, but I had to take my little sister Kim with us until Mom got off work when she would take Kim with her. Mom worked as a waitress in El Dorado. So here we are cruising the main drag with a three-year-old, having a blast. Ice cream cones do wonders to help amuse them.

We never really did any pranks; however, my junior year while jumping on the trampoline and attempting a back flip—Darren Brooks and Greg Eilert had been teaching me. But on that day, I tried it on my own and came crashing down on my neck. Crushed a disk and fractured a vertebrae, and I ended up in traction in the hospital in El Dorado for a week. Well, one day a bunch of my friends—Rosemary, Bruce Beem and several others, including my sister Michelle—showed up to hang out in my hospital room. It got rowdy and the nurses threw them out.

I wore a back brace for three months. However, just before Prom, I made it clear to the doctor that there was no way I was wearing a back brace to prom, wearing a halter formal. I went to prom without the brace.

March 17, 1977 was St. Patrick's Day, desecrated that year by the murder of Shirley Vian, BTK's sixth victim. It was right in the middle of the second semester of my junior year. Mom and Dad became very proactive in knowing where I would be going, when I would be going, and with whom I'd be going.

But, still, despite what was happening in Wichita, I was 17 and enjoying life. Wichita, after all, was still 45 minutes away. What was happening there simply was not happening in my world. And I wanted it to stay that way.

And then my world turned catawampus.

Catawampus AND cock-eyed.

They say that all good things come to an end. I wish *they* would've kept their mouths shut. Because, perhaps if they had shut up, maybe all the good things wouldn't have come to an end. Anyway, the happy days living in Potwin and going to Remington High School crashed to an end.

When my parents told me that we were moving back to Park City, I thought my world had ended. I wasn't going to get to graduate with my best friend Rosemary or other friends. Rosemary and I did everything together. We double-dated, were late for classes, got into all kinds of minor trouble. She was there on my first time getting to drive to El Dorado to cruise the drag.

Everything changed. With that move, now every time I would leave in the car or go anywhere, there was concern about crime; doors were locked; we had to worry about being mugged. Then there were the unsolved murders that I was beginning to learn about.

People in Park City and Wichita were scared. First there were the Otero murders, and then Kathryn Bright; and now Shriley Vian in the spring 1977. Other women were being killed that BTK was not bragging about. And then there were the women getting strangled out in California. Some people—probably a lot of people—wondered if the Hillside Strangler was going back and forth from California to Kansas, leaving strangled victims in his wake.

No longer did I wonder, *He wouldn't come to Potwin, would he?* Instead, I thought, *Hell, he might even live here in Park City.*

Rader candidly told the interviewing detectives that he had a thing for kids. "Yeah, a pedophile. Yeah. But I never—you know, the only thing I ever get closest to is Josephine, and I never had any sex with any kids or anything like that. But if the opportunity would arise as I got older . . . ."

Ten: In front of her kids

Out of all the surviving victims, the three that I felt whose lives were the most destroyed by Dennis were Charlie Otero, Gordon Wegerle, and Steven Relford.

Charlie had come home from school to find most of his family dead. He didn't have a fully restored relationship with other surviving members of his family until 2005—thirty-one years after the Otero murders.

I will talk more about Mr. Wegerle later. His wife Vicki was murdered in 1986. Police considered him a prime suspect for many years, the public assuming the worst and treating him like an abomination.

Steven was six years old when Dennis used a "russ" [ruse] on the unsuspecting boy prior to entering the home of Shirley Vian on March 17, St. Patrick's Day, 1977. He blamed himself all those years for what happened to his mother.

Those two boys—Charlie and Steven—whenever I saw them on TV, I would start to get tears in my eyes for their pain and loss of a decent future. Sure, a lot of people whom have never been through Post Traumatic Stress Disorder can sit there and judge and say, "Your life is what you make of it . . . ." I would like to see these same people try to do that after suffering something so traumatic. I hate to say it, because it sounds so trite, but it is easier said than done.

Shirley Vian was 26 when Dennis murdered her. He admitted during questioning that this was a random hit— he'd planned to kill someone else in the area, but his "project" was not at home.

She was survived by sons Junior Relford, 8, and Steven, 6; and daughter Stephanie Relford, 4.

This is what he told detectives about what happened on that St. Patrick's Day:

[Detectives asked him about the three-year break between the Bright and Vian murders. He compared the killing of human beings to fishing.]

I think it can be that a man goes fishing and sometimes he's not very lucky . . . it may be some social issues, busy at home or work. I'm sure that I was probably trolling and stalking, it just never—it just never happened.

I used the detective russ [ruse] on—that I was looking for somebody. I used the picture of a lady and a kid, to ask people if they—[the two in the picture]—if they lived in the neighborhood. That's when I talked to the Vian kid, when he came down from Dillons. I saw him coming. And I stopped him on the road and talked to him. You know, just like a stranger would. And then I saw where he went. And then I think I was already up to Black— Blackout's house [the home of his planned victim, who was not at home]. I followed the kid. I think I knocked . . . so I just went on in . . .

[Rader told detectives that the picture he showed the boy was actually of his wife and son. Then he bragged that he was well dressed that day.]

I was pretty spiffy looking. Dark slacks, regular dress shoes, and I had on an old, it was—had it made in Turkey. I was a—well, James Bond was real big back— back in the '60s. It was a James Bond style tweed sport coat . . . It's kind of like a spy thing. I had a briefcase. I had all my stuff in it. I already figured out what I was going to do, so I dressed . . . . I think I dressed at home. It was probably one of those days—that was St. Pat's Day. I think—I think they were having a parade downtown. My wife was probably at work.

Basically showed them the card and said I was a detective. I showed them my gun and they let me in. [Shirley Vian] was sick. She had a blue robe on, I think, and a pink—pink nightgown. And she had been in bed. I could tell she was sick . . . she was sick, she vomited once or twice, and I got her some water.

I tried to get control of the family. And there was two boys and a girl . . . did the same thing I did with the Brights: I said I was wanted, I did these things, you know. I like to take pictures and tie people up, you know.

Just to ease them that it's not going to be good for them, but they are going to get out of this alive, that I'm not really a real bad guy, until I get the control situation …I told them I was going to have to tie the kids up. She said, "Don't do that."

I said, "Yeah, I got to."

So when I tried to tie up the older boy first, he started to cry, which is understandable . . . I started tying him up, and he started to cry and fussing and whatever, and so I asked if we could put them somewhere . . . . Anyway, I tried to tie the kids up, and that didn't go, so we—we went ahead and moved [the three kids] into the bath-room. I must have tied the west bathroom door shot with the cord to—to the sink, I think. And then I tied the knots pretty tight so they couldn't get it [open].

I probably would have did the kids in like I did the Oteros and I probably would have hung the little girl. Like I said, I'm pretty mean—or could be. That's— but I—on the other hand, I'm very—you know, I'm a nice guy. I'm a nice guy, just, you know, it's one of those phases.

We [he and Shirley] took the bed and jammed that against it [bathroom door]. We put some toys and some blankets and stuff in there for them, books, going to make them comfortable, because I told them, "You guys stay in here." And I think one of them told me I was going to break out, and I said, "I don't think you want to, I'll shoot you, or blow your head off," or something like that. And they were upset.

I took her back to the back room, and we talked about what was going to happen, that I was going to tie her up and take pictures of her and then maybe have sex with her and she said, "Oh, I'm so sick."

I said, "As soon as we are done, we're out of here."

[He took her back to the bed they'd pushed against the bathroom door.]

I took her nighty off—her bathrobe and her nighty off, and I taped her hands. And then she got real sick, and maybe [I] taped her feet, because otherwise she could maybe run out the door, but I don't remember. But she needed some water. So I went to the kitchen and actually got a glass of water for her. And then she threw up, or she threw up before I got the water, one of the two.

[At one point the boys were able to push the door open enough to see what Rader was doing to their mother.]

The kids were banging on the door, trying to force the door open, and I could see them. It was probably the oldest one. He was looking there. He said, "Leave my mom alone! Leave my mom alone! Get out of here!"

He was trying to get out. I had already done it to her. [I'd] tied her ankles to that [bed]. Then I wrapped her neck real tight. I don't think I spent a lot of time strangling her, although I pulled it really tight, and I put a plastic bag over her head, wrapped it with her pink nighty. That was it.

I was excited. I didn't get to go full bore like I did on the Oteros. I didn't have time to do it. Christ. Then the phone rang. I remember the kid saying earlier that there was somebody going to check on us, [that] they are going to come over. I thought *Oh, gee, here it goes again*, that sort of thing you never know about. So that means somebody is going to come over, drive over or walk right over. *When are they going to be here? Are they going to be here right now?*

Plans change.

[He told detectives that he regretted not getting to kill the kids like he did the Oteros, and hang the little four-year-old girl.]

[I] grabbed something, a nighty or something, and wiped myself off, and zipped my pants up. Yeah, I grabbed a couple of pairs of underpants and headed out . . . went back and got the car and drove east of town and ditched some of my evidence.

Went back to a normal life.

[He envisioned Shirley Vian as his house servant in the afterlife.]

One of the reasons some people believe that Dennis' wife, Paula, had suspicions—at least as early as the aftermath of the Vian murder—is due to the following revelation that came out during those 32-plus hours of questioning after his arrest. He had written what he called the *Shirley* poem. His wife found a draft of that poem.

"What was really spooky," he said, "[was that] my wife almost found that [what he was really doing], because—I was doing AJ classes at [Wichita State University], and she found some of my damn cards that I made out, my draft cards. I stuck them down in the chair. I was working on some night, and she came in the house, and I stuck them down in the chair, and I forgot about them for some reason. And she found them and it scared— scared her. She said, 'Well, what's these?'

"I said, 'Well, we are working drafts because we are doing [the] BTK thing, whatever, you know, at school.'"

This is another thing I've wondered about. Did that experience cause Paula to have nightmares, or did she just let it wash off her back and one hundred percent accept her husband's explanation?

I'm not judging her. Just wondering.

Many times I've been asked what I think about Dennis Rader's ex-wife Paula. I don't believe that Paula could kill anybody, nor do I think she knew that Dennis was BTK; however, I do believe that she suspected him, because of his quirks. And, if she had known, I believe she would not have told because she wouldn't want to lose her standing with the community.

Eleven: When fear settled in

There was not a high school in Park City, so I attended Wichita Heights High School, which Dennis had attended years before. I settled into a routine of going to school in the morning and then working evenings at Spencer Gifts at Towne East Mall.

It was like there was a chill of fear in the air. I dearly missed the comfortable, safe feeling I had when we lived in Potwin.

Warnings from Dad and Mom were more strident, and they came more often.

"Keep your doors locked. Don't pick up strangers. Don't drink. Don't drive fast. Be aware of your surroundings. You girls be careful."

Real fear was creeping into my life. People really got scared after the strangulation death of Nancy Fox on December 9, 1977.

I heard the report on rock and roll station KEYN while driving to work. I remembered another woman who'd been murdered walking to the laundry mat. A creepy feeling ran up my spine. When I arrived at work, the jewelry manager at Spencer's—she was dating a Wichita Police Officer at the time—instructed the girls to walk each other to our cars, and if they weren't parked close by each other, then we were to drive each other to our cars.

When we weren't busy at work, we would talk about the murders and wonder when it was going to be safe again, each of us hoping we wouldn't be a victim.

Do I believe Dennis Rader killed more than ten people? I personally don't think this was all.

There are still unsolved murders that occurred on the same days of the week that most of his victims were murdered.

I mean, do all murders occur on Tuesdays, Thursdays, and Saturdays? Is there some rule book for murderers which says that you can only kill on these days?

Twelve: His "perfect hit"

Can you imagine a guy getting a hard on while being questioned by detectives? According to an except in the court filing, THE STATE OF KANSAS vs. DENNIS L. RADER, it happened while Wichita Police Detective Tim Relph discussed a picture with Dennis that he'd drawn of Nancy Fox.

RADER: That's pretty accurate, I did if from memory.

DET. RELPH: Did you do this with the intention of sending this in, or did you just do this for your own consumption?

RADER: Part of the media thing, and also sexual …I'm sorry, guys, [but] I'm getting a hard on looking at it right now. I'm sorry.

DET. RELPH: We'll take care of that. (He took the picture away.)

I'm thinking for the umpteenth time during the sentencing hearing, *What a sicko. What did I ever do to deserve being sentenced to be supervised by this sorry excuse of a human for six-and-one-half years?*

There's no going back, but you can go forward. I read or heard somewhere that *Today is the very first day of the rest of my life.* I've learned to live my life that way, literally one day at a time, knowing that each twenty-four hours puts more time separation between me and that *Evil.* It helps knowing he's spending his days and nights in an 8 by 10-foot cubicle.

Unfortunately, his fantasies are still fueled by thoughts of what he called his "perfect hit".

Nancy Fox was 25 when Dennis killed her. His discussion of victim number seven came across more like he was reminiscing than confessing.

Here's what he said:

Project Foxhunt. Fox went the way I wanted it. I was in complete control. I didn't have anybody bothering me, so I did that the way I wanted to do it.

[He said the apartment next to her place was vacant so no one would hear any screams.]

Nancy Fox, I had a lot of control on that. That was what I call a perfect . . . a perfect hit, although she gave me a lot of verbal static, but she cooperated, and didn't fight me. You know, she didn't raise a big ruckus and scream or anything like that.

I [had] followed her a couple of times. I checked her mailbox, went out to Helzberg's where she worked...I actually saw her. She really appealed to me as a sexual female victim. So I probably had an attachment with her . . . more than I did on the others.

[His wife expected him to be at the library on the night he murdered Nancy.]

That particular night, I had WSU, and I just left. I knew I had a time frame, I knew when she got home. I had to get there and get in the house. I parked a few blocks away, like I done on some others.

I wanted to make sure she wasn't in there. I went to the front door and knocked. I was going to use, "I'm sorry, wrong apartment, I was looking for Joanne," or something. Then hopefully, I would show her the weapon and step in.

I went back around...I thought I was pretty well hid. I went through the window, pried it open and went on in.

Nancy was a really—a nice person. She dressed nice, she had nice neat stuff. And the way it was all laid out and stuff, it looked like she's, you know, she was a nice family girl. Leave it to a weird buy like me to do that.

[She found Dennis in the kitchen when she arrived home.]

She said, "Well you get out of my house. I'm going to call the police."

And I said, "It won't do you any good. I already cut the phone line." Or I said, "I already fixed the phone."

She was pretty feisty. She said, "I got to have a smoke. What are you in the house for?"

Just like I told some of the others, I was basically a bad guy, I just wanted sex, and take some pictures of you, tie you up.

I said, "I have to tie you up to take pictures."

She said, "You don't have to do that."

I said, "Yeah, I do…"

[Dennis dumped her purse's contents out on the kitchen table while Nancy smoked a cigarette.]

I got her driver's license and some other stuff out of there.

She said, "Let's get this over with. What are you going to do?"

"Well, I'm probably going to rape you. I'm going to tie you up."

"Do you have to tie me up?"

"Yeah."

"You're sick."

"Yeah, I'm sick, ma'am," but, I said, "that's the way it's got to be."

She said, "Oh, my God, get out of here," and all that kind of stuff.

She asked me about my gloves and the handcuffs. I said, "That's part of my deal. I got to have them or it won't work."

She said, "This is ridiculous." Then she says [in his voice mimicking her] "Yada, yada, yada . . . . This is a bunch of bullshit."

[He allowed her to go to the bathroom, telling her to not have much clothes on when she came out. He made sure she couldn't lock the door. She came out wearing a sweater, bra, and panties.]

I told her to lay down...I had a belt, and wrapped it around her legs...I just took that up and wrapped it around her neck. I pulled her underpants down. I was basically nude or pretty close to nude at that time. I crawled on top of her. The belt that I used was the belt I was wearing. I just took it off when I took my clothes off and had it.

[He strangled her with the belt.]

I had her come back, and I whispered in her ear a little bit. I told her I was BTK. I was a bad guy. And then she really squirmed and then—I pulled—put the pressure down on it.

I loosened up a little bit...because I was going to put some panty hose on, she came back and that's when I whispered in her ear, told her who I was. I don't know if she made the connection or not, but she wasn't happy with that, I yanked her up, tightened it and took her on.

She never did fight. Verbally she wasn't happy. "I'm going to call the police," and I was sick.

No, I had complete control of her, that's why it was one of the more—more enjoyable kills, as I call them.

When I was strangling her . . . . Yeah, she did grab a hold of my nuts, she was squeezing pretty hard. But it actually made it more excited. I mean, she actually started digging in. She clawed me up pretty good down there.

I was on a high. I remember I was really on a high. I took a nighty that was there, and I masturbated in it and left it there.

Nancy will be a primary mistress in the afterlife. She will obey my bondage conditions.

[Dennis fed off the publicity. When he had heard or seen nothing in the news the next day about the murder of Nancy Fox, he made a phone call.]

[It was] a bold move...probably a stupid bold move. Probably a thing you do when you're younger, and if you think things out you wouldn't do it. [I] was still on a high. I wanted to get something going, something in the paper. Excitement. Yeah, I get a bit of excitement reading about stuff in the paper, that's why I've been on a media frenzy. You know, you sit there and they talk about you on TV, it's—that's pretty high type stuff. I don't know whether you call it a sick mind or not. I've always paid real close attention to the media.

[Dennis called from a pay phone outside a market. He talked first to the operator.]

You will find a homicide at 843 South Pershing, Nancy Fox.

[He asked the operator for the emergency number to the police department. The operator contacted the dispatcher. The dispatcher asked the caller to repeat the address and the operator interrupted. "He gave 843 South Pershing."

Dennis said, "That is correct" and left the phone off the hook.]

I can't get Dan Lickey's statement out of my mind...that the reason Dennis had escaped detection for so many years was "Plain dumb luck." Here he called from a public pay phone and did not disguise his voice. A recording probably was made . . . yet no one ever associated the voice with Dennis.

If Dennis had a guardian angel, I'm convinced that angel wore black.

My friends and I soon started traveling in packs for security. At times there would be ten or twelve of us riding and arriving together, and we stayed close to each other. Male friends that went with us kept a close eye on us. Very rarely did we dance with anyone other than those in our own group.

Thirteen: Disco fever

In January 1978—one month before my 18th birthday—I started going to the discos, using an ID from one of the girls I worked with. I was damn sure that in that eternity of a month, that life was going to pass by and, by gosh, I was not going to miss out.

I'd get off work, call Mom and tell some made-up story that I was going to catch a movie and a snack with my cousin, who was three years older. I would listen to Mom's standard lecture—don't do this . . . don't do that... keep your doors locked.

"Yes, Mom," I'd reply, and then head for Star Baby's, a local disco palace of polyester, disco haircuts and boogie fever—where Tony Manero flew in on Tuesdays to dance, leaving the paint store and 2001 Odyssey in Bay Ridge, Brooklyn—to meet up with my cousin there. Actually, Star Baby's was a bar, more attuned to us and our culture than Tony Manero and the anger-ridden culture of 2001 Odessey would have been. And we didn't have to have a lighted plexiglass dance floor to enjoy ourselves, either.

I'd get behind the wheel, and that's when the jitters would set in. Driving at night, alone in a 1966 Chevy Nova station wagon, I'd get really creeped out in that vehicle with all those windows, shadows bouncing off the glass, sometimes causing me to hold my breath, other times shocking me close to hyperventilation.

Many times I'd be driving down the road when the hair on my body would stand up, and I'd get the feeling that there was someone lying in the floorboard of the backseat. I could hear my heart race, and just knew if there were someone back there, he could read my thoughts, and he'd know that I knew.

I'd hold my breath as I'd reach up to pull the rearview mirror down to give me a view of the backseat, which, of course, didn't work, and then I'd pull into a gas station and get out of the car, walk around to get a good look in the windows. It'd become a ritual—even if I'd thoroughly checked the car before leaving work.

Finally, after I took several deep breaths, it was off to the festivities at the bar.

My friends and I soon started traveling in packs for security. At times there would be ten or twelve of us riding and arriving together, and we stayed close to each other. Male friends that went with us kept a close eye on us. Very rarely did we dance with anyone other than those in our own group.

Adding to our fears were the murders happening out in California. We speculated that maybe the Hillside Strangler was going back and froth from California, leaving bodies in his wake. It *did* have to be a he didn't he? No woman could have done all that.

But then the seven serial murders of Aileen Wuornos in 1990 were still a dozen years off.

Also on our minds was an urban legend—although we didn't know what an urban legend was at the time—going around that a man was hiding under women's cars and, while a woman was getting into her car, the man would use a knife to cut the back of her ankle to prevent her from running, and then he would rape and murder her.

Although BTK would confess to three more murders committed during the next thirteen years, fear and anxiety were at peak level in 1977 and 1978. I've never experienced anything like it before or since.

I went often to the drive-in movies, also traveling in a crowd. Sometimes that crowd included my younger brother Hobert and a younger cousin, Jerry, both then about 14; plus my friend Nancy's younger brother in the trunk of a car so we wouldn't have to pay admission for them. We put the saved money toward beer and Swisher Sweet Cigars.

We'd also cruise four-lane Douglas Street that runs east and west through Wichita's downtown, along with other bumper-to-bumper cars loaded with teenagers out looking to have a good time.

Although the teens would yell at one another and visit from car to car, it was the college and older guys that we were careful to stay away from, because no one knew who was doing the killings.

Every time I went out—even during the day—I was always looking in the rearview mirror; and when I stopped at a red light and there was a man in the car next to me who looked in my direction, I'd get scared and wonder if that was HIM, and if I'd be next.

I quit school that January and got my GED.

When I turned 18, I wanted to join the Air Force. Dad got really upset and told me that the Air Force wouldn't take me because I wasn't smart enough. That comment burrowed into my craw and stayed. I wanted to do recon work in the Air Force, and forever after regretted that I didn't believe in myself enough to ignore Dad's harsh words.

Had I joined, I believe I would have made a career out of it. It remains one of the *What ifs . . .* that litter my past.

Dennis Rader wrote a poem, celebrating the suffering he had inflicted on Nancy Fox:

"Oh! Death to Nancy"

"I'll stuff your jaws till you can't talk.
I'll bind your legs till you can't walk.
I'll tie your hands till you can't make a stand.
And finally I'll close your eyes so you can't see.
I'll bring sexual death unto you for me."

Fourteen: Factor X

BTK was always doing something near my birthday—at least, to me, it seemed that way. He exposed his gigantic ego again in a four-page document postmarked February 9, 1978 he sent to KAKE Television, which was received on February 10—eight days after my 18th birthday.

Looking back, I can only ask myself, *"Why am I not surprised?"* His ego showed so much at times when he supervised me in the Park City Compliance Department that I wondered how he could get out of his chair, the weight of his ego was so huge.

He just could not get enough of himself.   Publicity made him feel important, like he'd achieved things no one else had. He felt he was smarter than the police. He was invincible. In his mind, getting away with murder for so many years just proved it. He, therefore, had license to taunt the police, berate the media, and terrorize the good citizens of Wichita and Park City.

It's a cliché, but it is true: *Dennis was a legend in his own mind.* He relived over and over his despicable deeds for self-gratification.   He wanted everybody to celebrate and savor his deeds, marvel at his genius.

The truth is just as Jeff Davis, the son of Delores Davis—BTK's 10th victim, told Dennis to his face on the second day of the sentencing hearing: "You are as lucky as you are dumb."

Anyway, Dennis couldn't stand it that the media had not shared his poem about Shirley Vian with the public. He'd mailed it January 31 to the *Eagle Beacon* news-paper. Ironically, the poem had been placed in the dead letter file when *Eagle Beacon* employees thought it was a Valentine that arrived without payment.

Here's a snippet from the short poem he called *Shirley Locks*:

". . . thou shalt not screem nor yet fee the line, but lay on cushion and think of me and death and how its going to be."

This is exactly the wording and spelling BTK used. It was believed to have been taken from the poem *Curly Locks*, which had recently been published in *Games*, a word puzzle magazine. Dennis would later deny that.

His poem *Oh! Death to Nancy* was also in the four-page document.

"I'll stuff your jaws till you can't talk.

I'll bind your legs till you can't walk.

I'll tie your hands till you can't make a stand.

And finally I'll close your eyes so you can't see.

I'll bring sexual death unto you for me."

He spelled poorly. He actually wrote *blind* for bind and *leg's* for legs. His command of the English language was awkward both then and during the six-and-one-half years I worked under his supervision. How he got his degree from WSU I have no idea. He admitted to detectives that he had not been a good student.

In that four-page document, Dennis showed his frustration with the lack of media attention. "How many do I have to Kill before I get a name in the paper or some national attention," he wrote.

Then he chided law enforcement for supposedly not seeing the connection between the Otero, Vian, Fox, and another unnamed, murders. "Do the cop [sic] think that all those deaths are not related? Golly-gee, yes the M.O. is different in each, but look a pattern is developing."

He confirmed that the Vian children were lucky to be alive. "A phone call save them. I was go-ng [sic] to tape the boys and put plastic bag over their head like I did Joseph, and Shirley. And then hang the girl. God oh God what a beautiful sexual relief that would been . . . Josephine, when I hung her really turn me on, her pleading for mercy then the rope took hold, she helpless, staring at me with wide terror fill eyes the rope getting tighter-tighter."

Dennis said other serial killers had "Factor X" and used that as an excuse for the murders. He did not explain what "Factor X" was. "I don't lose any sleep over it. After a thing like Fox I come home and go about life like anyone else."

He suggested the media might call him "The B.T.K. Strangler . . . Its time: 7down [sic] and many more to go."

If his plan was to keep people on edge, Dennis succeeded.

During the time I was going to discos, a lot of silly jokes were going around. These are the only two I remember:

Have you read the book *Sitting in the bleachers* by Seymour Butts?

Do you know what you call a dog in the water without legs? Bob.

Fifteen: A great summer

Around March I stopped going to discos and started going to regular bars that played Country and Southern Rock music. By the end of 1978 I'd quit going to bars. And I'd gotten married. But that was still several months in the future.

I was at my friend Rosemary's house the day after she graduated from Remington High School in May. She had her bags packed, and she moved to Park City to live with my parents and us. She got a job along with Michelle and me at Dobb's House at the airport, where we also worked with my cousin Vickie. We were waitresses on second shift, 2 p.m. to 10 p.m.

We always carried clothes with us to change into so that as soon as we got off work we would head for the bars and go dancing or go to friends' houses. I was dating the man that I'd marry later that year. Russ Hamm would father my daughter Krissy.

It was a great summer, highlighted by my August marriage.

Unfortunately, the marriage went the way so many marriages do when both partners marry so young. Neither of us was really ready for the sudden responsibilities. It wasn't so much that we fell out of love, I think, as it was the fact that we fell into a kind of boredom that gradually wore us out.

Krissy was the lasting treasure my first marriage produced.

I adore all three of my children. Kyle and Trent were the treasures resulting from my second marriage, a very unsettling union that lasted from 1986 into 1991.

Let me flash forward, because I love to talk about my kids.

Krissy and I are both Tom Jones fans, and dream of someday getting to Las Vegas to see him in concert.

She has three children of her own. I get plenty of baby-sitting, bonding time with them.

In high school Krissy was in debate, forensics, drama, choir, a cheerleader and on dance squad, plus she held down a job to pay for her own car insurance and gas. She let me know whenever she had competition, but when she performed she would never look at me, because I would be crying from pride, and it would cause her to make mistakes.

My children will tell you that if I could, I would still give them a curfew until they were 50, and still make them check in. Krissy once told me that she knew that I was tough when she was younger, but wanted to thank me, because she could have ended up a mess. Instead, she's a wife, mother, career woman, and everyday she works hard to succeed. She told me once that she wanted to be the career woman that she saw in me when I was working for Pinkerton. She said that I was confident, determined, and I knew how to handle problems—that she was modeling herself after me, the way I was before I went to work for Park City and started to deteriorate.

It felt good to hear this from her. Sometimes we need to hear that our children were and are proud of us.

Both my boys are wonderful, and the best part being that they are alike, yet so different, which allows me to have separate relationships with both.

I will share an anecdote about the time Kyle was living with me in Park City, but that will have to wait until a later chapter. During the time I was writing this book, he was Corporal Kyle Lloyd USMC, driving a tank in Iraq.

My younger son Trent is a real charmer, and every-one loves him. He stands 6"3", and weighs about 180 pounds. Our joke between my boys and myself is that I tell them, "Don't make me get a ladder so that I can slap you." Then we bust up laughing. One, because of the joke; and two, because I probably only ever struck my three children once or twice in their lifetime, but I can yell! That's another joke between the boys. I won't hit them, but I can sure scare the hell out of them when I raise my voice, that's when they know I mean business.

I have great children—they're smart, they're beautiful, they're polite, respectful. And there is one other thing, they're smartasses like their mother, all three of them.

I love 'em.

Rebecca Chavez, 24-year-old granddaughter of Anna Williams, often stayed the night at 615 South Pinecrest because of her employment. On April 28, 1979, Rebecca was called into work and did not stay at her grandmother's house as planned.

Had she done so, Rebecca very likely would have become BTK's eighth murder victim.

And had her grandmother not gone out square dancing that night, there might have been two victims. When she arrived home, Anna noticed that the door to her spare bedroom was open. A vanity drawer was open and clothes were on the floor. In her bedroom she found empty jewelry boxes and clothes missing from the drawer.

Anna hurried to the phone to call police, but the line was dead. She rushed to the home of a neighbor, who called the police.

On June 15, 1979, Anna received an envelope containing a poem, a drawing of a nude bound woman, a scarf, and a piece of jewelry—it was her scarf and jewelry.

Police recognized the symbol in the right hand corner of the enclosed letter.

Sixteen: Beyond despicable

While alternating between watching and listening to the sentencing hearing, I thought it couldn't be possible for Dennis to sink deeper into depravity. I was proven wrong during testimony about the murder of Marine Hedge. She was killed on the night of April 27, 1985—three-and-one-half months after my 25th birthday.

I lived with my parents in Park City at the time. This was right after my divorce of Russ, and I was trying to get back on my feet. The murder occurred just about a block from my grandparents' house.

Marine was a five-foot-two, 100-pound middle-aged lady who lived four houses down the street from where Dennis lived. In carrying out "Project Cookie" he went far beyond despicable.

You will see what I mean when you read it in Dennis' own words.

She just lived up the street. So I could watch out of the house and see when she came home. Usually later in the evening after it was dark.

I knew she worked at the hospital, Wesley. I had been at that cafeteria. We waved to her as a neighbor …worked in coffee shop at the hospital . . . 2 p.m. to midnight. So I thought, *Can I really pull this off? Can I really pull this off right close to my house and get away with it? Ooh, this will be a biggy if I can.*

It was really bad for a guy that knocks one of [the] neighbors off. That's not good for a serial killer, because you don't want to kill in your own habitat. That's a bad sign. This is not really good serial killer business; this is right at my back door.

She was probably one of my most complicated hits. Layout . . . I used a taxi . . . did a lot of maneuverment

[sic] to get to her, you know, it's not one of those where you just drive up and walk up.

It was a cubby thing [a Cub Scout outing]. It's a good cover for a guy like me to go out and camp out and slip away after everybody goes to bed, or park somewhere different than everybody. And that's what I basically did that night. And it was muddy. It had rained a lot and it was muddy. So to make sure that I got out of there, I told them I had a headache or something. I said I'm going to bed early.

...got in the car and drove over to Andover and put on all—I call it my hit, the hit clothes, you know, darker . . . just pulled back here on a country road. Now I had to completely—I had my stuff, so I had to completely get dressed for my...hit. I could still stuff more in pockets and be more flexible than my scout stuff.

[Dennis then drove to a bowling alley.]

So I parked my car at the bowling alley, and pretend that I'm really having a good time. I go in and order a beer. And I don't drink it, just put some on my face and I splash a little on my clothes so the taxicab driver that picks me up knows I've been drinking, and he can smell it. And that's my russ [ruse].

I planned to tell the driver, "The guys and I have been out partying...I need somebody to drive me home." [He'd put his stuff in a bowling ball bag. He told the driver to let him out on the next street over from Independence, the street on which he and Marine Hedge lived.]

I told the driver, "I need to exercise, I need to walk." I said, "I need to walk this off . . . I need to walk a little bit." Because I talked in kind of a slurred voice...and pretending that I was drunk, but I wasn't.

I already knew the park; there was a park back there. Actually went through my in-law's yard [His wife Paula's parents lived two houses over from their house, and two houses from Marine Hedge's place—right in the middle.]

. . . because they have an open back yard. So I went through there, cut through there and then back to her house.

I thought she was home because her car was there. I cut the phone lines and I did it like a cat burglar thing. Very quiet. It took me a long time to get in the house. It's pretty hard to get in a house and be really quiet. I crept in there really, really quiet, and then she wasn't there.

I thought, *Oh shoot. The car is there but she's not there. Where in the hell is she at?*

At about the time I got that all figured out, I could hear a male voice and a car door slam. I didn't like to confront males after the Bright thing. And I wasn't too thrilled with that on the Otero thing, although that did go—I mean, I controlled them—I controlled things on that, but I didn't control the thing on Bright. That was two young guys—two young kids; they fought like hell.

I thought, *If I can avoid it, I'm not going to go with the male thing. If it is, it's going to be quick, I'm not going to mess around with strangling them...I'm just going to shoot them or knife them.*

[Dennis went into a bedroom closet and hid until the male friend left.]

I stayed in that closet a long, long time . . . he left . . . waited and waited [some more] until I thought she was in bed. She was asleep until I jumped on her bed. She started to scream. I put my mitt . . . I put a hand over her mouth real quiet like. I wanted to tie her up and take some pictures and do the sexual fantasy thing with her.

She said, "What in the hell's going on? . . . yada, yada, yada."

She probably thought she was going to be raped or something.

I got her under control.

She tried to fight me as well as she could, she made some sounds. I was right on top of her. There wasn't any way . . . she was a smaller lady, so there's no way that she could really fight me. I just went ahead and throttled her right there. I throttled her until I got control of her, and then I handcuffed her and then I finished her off...strangled her with a belt or something, but I think I throttled her [with my hands].

I went ahead and stripped her there, and wrapped her up in her blankets and stuff. Went out to her car and popped the trunk.

Marie [He sometimes called her "Marine" and sometimes "Marie."] Hedge was my first one I ever dealt with a dead body. I couldn't believe how even a small lady, how heavy she was. That's how I got her to the car, drug [sic] her out to the car and put her in the trunk.

What I was going to do was kidnap her, take her out to a barn. I had a barn rigged up where I had some black plastic. I have a thing with barns. When I was younger, I used to kill animals in barns like cats and dogs. Usually it was stray cats—I would take them in there and hang them or wrap them up in bailing wire or something. Just one of those things I did.

This ain't going to do it, guys. This ain't honest, that's what I would like—but, actually I took her to the church, okay? Because when you guys get the pictures, which you will find, you are going to say, well, that's not a barn.

[He was referring to Christ Lutheran Church—the same church where years later the membership would elect him as their congregation president . . . and the same church where his wife Paula sang in the choir.]

Hillside, right across from Heights [High School] . . . it's been torn down now . . . there's a new [building].

I had the plastic hid already at the church. That's premeditated. I was a congregational member over there. Rolls of plastic, black plastic and the thumb tacks .

. . taped that window off. I even went outside to make sure you couldn't see any light.

Her alive or dead, she was going to that church . . . took some pictures of her and put her in bondage things at the church. And I had my time with her.

I basically photographed her in bondage . . . with her hands behind her back. She was dead. You guys will probably find the pictures sooner or later in my archives of her, different poses of her.

Daylight was coming up. *Oh shoot, I got to hurry.* Panic was starting to set in . . . *I got to get this all done and cleaned up and get out of here. I got to get back to the car, get back to the scout place.*

I just took her back to the east until I thought I found a nice place and dumped her [in a drainage ditch and covered the body with brush. He had used Marine Hedge's car that night and early morning].

I thought, *Gee, I wish I had this car* [a Monte Carlo] *I wish it was mine.*

I was soaking with sweat . . . returned to the church and cleaned up. The time was pushing on me, because I had to get back to the scout place at 7:30 or eight (a.m.), so I was in a hurry.

I left the cord with her. After I left—started to clear my evidence. I said, I need to get that cord. That cord evidence. If you get the cord then they'll know it's someone else. I went back Monday when I was going back to work, and I purposely left early so I would make sure I got there, and—and I had a little trouble finding her, and—you know, because the brush and stuff; it was really dark. Because when I dropped her off it was daylight and I could see. And the odor was—she had already started to decompose. I found the cord and I got it out as quick as I could.

And then—and then I used a pair of different boots so I wouldn't leave footprints or I changed those when I got in the car. I was very careful about that.

Marine Hedge was a friendly neighbor. We wouldn't visit, but we would wave to each other and she would say, "Hi."

[It's as I said] . . . really bad for a guy that knocks one of the neighbors off.

I don't recall Dennis revealing his afterlife plans for Marine Hedge, and I think he came up with "Project Cookie" because of a comment he made during his confession that the houses in his neighborhood looked like *cookie cutter* homes.

In an ironic twist, Dennis actually calmed down some neighbors who concluded that Marine's boyfriend had killed her.

It nauseated me, hearing the word images of him strangling a nice lady, hauling her nude body into a church, no less, and then putting her body into different bondage poses just so he could take photos for later sexual release.

And this is the guy who became my boss.

Self-bondage almost got Dennis in trouble.

"Yeah, on one of my last campouts, I got myself in a bad jam; I thought I was going to have to get—to yell to have one of the kids come over and get me, one of the people there.

"It was really embarrassing—it would have been embarrassing."

Rader escaped and spared himself the embarrassment of having Cub Scouts free him from his self-bondage.

"Yeah, it took me an hour, but I did it. And I was really—and I had slipped on a—a pair of—well, they were—they were choke chains on dogs. But, you know, what's—what's funny, you know—I didn't bagged this stuff up. Ten minutes later, I masturbated."

Seventeen: Something in common

Isn't it weird that Dennis and I both worked for a company in the security field prior to working for Park City?

I think it is.

ADT Security Services released this statement on February 28, 2005:

> ADT Security Services shares in the community's relief that police in Wichita have arrested a suspect in connection with a string of murders dating back more than 30 years.
>
> It is because of the recent arrest over the weekend and the associated news stories that ADT became aware of Dennis Rader as a suspect.
>
> We can confirm that Rader was an ADT employee who left the company about 16 years ago. Because his employment ended so many years ago, detailed information is more difficult to obtain. Our initial search shows that he was employed from November 1974 to July 1988 in our Wichita, Kansas branch office.
>
> ADT intends to fully cooperate with any investigation.

Compare the way ADT handled their statement with the official response of Park City:

> Due to an ongoing criminal investigation, the City of Park City can answer no questions pertaining to Dennis Rader. The Open Records Laws of the State of Kansas provide that only the following information can be made public upon request: Name, Job Title, Rate of Pay, and Date of Hire.

Mayor Emil Bergquist

I wondered then—and still do now—why Bergquist did not acknowledge that he and the City of Park City were also fully cooperating with any investigation. Could it be that he felt upstaged by the Wichita Police Department—that THEY, and not the Park City Police Department—had pulled off the coup of arresting BTK, and were basking in the international spotlight?

The day the Wichita Police Department arrived to arrest Dennis Rader was a black eye to the Park City Police Department. They were kept out of the loop in their own front yard. The rest of the world sees it the way it is. That must have been a blow to their God Complex.

Anyway, as I was saying, I find it weird that we both had jobs with security companies—Dennis with ADT Security Services, and me with Pinkerton Security & Investigations.

I worked 13 years for Pinkerton, 1984 to 1997. Eventually I was promoted to Assistant Operations Manager, assigned to the company's office in Carson, California. After returning to Kansas, I worked as an auditor for corporate operations. When it reached the point where I was traveling constantly and felt like I was working 48 hours a day and never getting to see my children, I quit.

Dennis was highly curious about what I did for Pinkerton. I'll tell you about it in chapter twenty-one.

When Vicki Wegerle was murdered, I was roommates with my friend Penny and my sister Michelle in Wichita.

After Marine Hedge's murder, people up and down the street trimmed back bushes and plants to make it harder for anyone to sneak around their homes unobserved.

And what did Dennis do?

Nothing.

You could hardly see the front of his house. But then, he did not have the same fears his neighbors had.

Eighteen: Project Piano

Vicki Wegerle was murdered on September 16, 1986. One of the real tragedies in the wake of her death is that suspicion lingered many years in the minds of detectives and others that husband Gordon had killed his wife. That cloud of suspicion did not lift until seventeen-and-a-half years later when the officially "cold case" thawed out with a most unexpected confession from BTK on March 19, 2004.

I remember that day very well, and will discuss it in detail in a later chapter. It was just a few weeks before Dennis locked the door and barred my only exit from our office in City Hall.

If ever there was a man deeply in love with his wife, it was Gordon Wegerle. I can't imagine the depth of his sorrow compounded by the fact that he didn't kill his wife, yet others refused to believe him.

On the other hand, I know exactly what it feels like to tell people the truth and then have your words fall on deaf ears. That's why I wrote this book, so I could tell the truth, especially about what happened to me during and after the six-and-one-half years I worked under Dennis Rader's supervision in the Compliance Department in Park City.

I still blame myself for not figuring out he was BTK before he was arrested. Like my psychologist told me, the nightmares represented an attempt by my subconscious to warn me of danger—I just didn't associate that Dennis was THAT danger. I did, however, increasingly sense the evil in Dennis.

Here's what he said about Vicki Wegerle, who was a loving mother still in her 20's when her life was stolen.

Just saw her. Saw her either get out of the car or drive up in the car and walk.

[He said he watched her about three weeks.]

The more I knew about the person, I felt the better [sic] because I tried to be, I guess what you would call professional in the matter. I didn't want to get caught.

I would come out in the evening, kind of walk around. I could hear she played a piano, so she became Project Piano. I hear[d] the piano. I thought, *Well, that would be a good code name for her.*

[Remember, he worked for ADT Security.]

The company was going through a management problem: they had been bought out by a corporate raider from England, and we didn't—the employees really didn't know what the hell was going on. But anyway, our bosses were—a lot of times they were gone. And so what is the theory? When the cat is away the mice will play

I took a Southwestern Bell manual; they have the emblem on the front, and I just trimmed that down and taped it on the top of my hat. As a bogie, bogie hat . . . A yellow hard hat . . . opens a lot of doors for you. I flipped the helmet on and had the briefcase, and walked across the street . . . and went to the east house first. There was an older couple, I think, in there. And I told them I was—we had been doing a telephone repair work, and we needed to check the cables inside the house, the connectors inside the house, because of static and stuff.

Why [did I do that]? Because I think if—if I walked across the street, and I walk right to your house, you're going to say, "Gee, why is he walking to my house?"

I got there, I heard the piano. I came in the house, and told her [Vicki Wegerle] I needed to check the telephone terminals.

She said, "They are over there."

I maybe small talked to her.

And her kid was there. And the little kid was there in the play pen . . . she was even on the piano when I got there, because I heard the piano

She had a dining room table pretty close to the telephone terminal. I laid my stuff up there. I had a little . . . tester thing. I went over there and monkeyed around with it, and then I said, "Well, it looks like it works."

I pulled out my gun. I said, "Let's go to the bedroom."

She got really upset and started crying and everything. She said, "How about my kid?"

I said, "I don't know about your kid."

She said, "My husband is going to be home pretty soon."

I said, "Well, I hope he's not going to be home too soon."

At that time I was experimenting with leather, trying to tie her up with leather, or shoe strings, leather up, you know.

I laid her on the bed, and she was crying and upset. She broke the bonds then she started fighting with me. We fought really hard. We rolled on the bed, and we rolled on the floor. We were all over the place. She was fighting for her life, and I was trying to take her down.

She fought like a hell cat, too. In fact, I think she nicked me . . . I know you guys . . . you got some stuff on her fingernails. I probably still have the scratch somewhere on my face if you looked.

I think I grabbed—she either had a nylon sock or a sock in there . . . I finally got her down . . . nylon stocking—wrapped it around her neck.

The dogs were barking and the windows were open. I thought her husband was going to walk in. I said, *This is a real nice mess.* I really didn't have time...And then I stuffed that [gag] in her, pulled her pants down a little farther and took some quick pictures.

I should have done a hit earlier in the day. [Her] husband coming home mess [sic] things up and timing. After the fight and death didn't have time to enjoy it.

As I was leaving here, the EMS was heading that way. I knew what that was for . . . then I drove all the way out to the west part of town, I got rid of my evidence.

Vicki will be one of my slave bondage women in the afterlife.

In one of many ironic twists in the BTK saga, while driving home to have lunch with his wife, Gordon Wegerle passed Dennis, who was driving the opposite direction behind the wheel of Vicki's 1978 gold Chevy Monte Carlo.

Gordon at first thought it was his wife's car, but brushed aside the notion when he noticed a man driving the car. It was not until he reached home and saw the empty driveway that he realized he really had seen his wife's car.

Minutes late to try and save his wife's life, he was emotionally shattered.

Then a disbelieving public picked at the pieces.

Dennis told the detectives interviewing him that he thought he would never get caught, that he had plans for an eleventh victim.

"If you guys hadn't caught me, I might have pulled it off . . . final curtain call. I was basically going to do this like a play production. I was going to write a list of characters, you know, and, you know, down at the bottom *BTK Productions*, or something like that—some wild thing like that. It was basically going to have all you guys, anybody that ever ran in the paper that had any connection, your name was going to show up in there and what—basically you did. Like—Ken, you know, the main BTK investigator. All the way back, you know, boom."

Nineteen: "Another one prowls..."

Apparently, Dennis—in his mind—considered himself a connoisseur of fine murders—even those committed by someone else. However, in reality, I believe the murders of Melvin Fager and his daughters, Sherri, 10; and Kelli, 16, merely gave him an excuse to inflict mental torture on Mary Fager, the bereaved spouse and mother.

Also, of course, to taunt police with another reminder that BTK was still around.

Mrs. Fager had returned to her Wichita home from an out-of-town trip in late December 1987. Her husband had been shot twice in the back. Sherri, wearing pajamas, had been drowned in the hot tub. Kelli had been strangled, and her nude body placed in the hot tub several hours after Sherri.

An envelope, postmarked January 5, 1988, was delivered to Mrs. Fager. The envelope contained a poem titled *Oh God He Put Kelli Sherri in the Tub* and a drawing of a young nude girl bound at the wrists and ankles, lying next to what could either be a pool or hot tub.

The poem's author did not take credit for the murders.

"Another one prowls the deep abyss of lewd thoughts and deeds."

Rader told detectives that he had admired the man that murdered the Fagers.

"If the girls were bound with black plastic tape and drowned, that's pretty sexual in my category. That's hot stuff in my category. That's—that's some sexual activity. You know, you know, if they were nude that was even more so. You know, to do that, you got to control the victim, make them take their clothes off and bind them and drown them. You know, that's got some sexual overtones. That's the kind of stuff—that's the kind of stuff that I would do or the kind of stuff that I like to collect. Sorry."

A local contractor was arrested and charged with the Fager murders. He had been doing construction work for Mr. Fager. He said he'd gone to the Fager house and discovered the father's body, had heard some noise in the house and fled in the family's car. Apprehended in Florida four days later, the man claimed he had a total blank of the events that had occurred. A jury acquitted him of all charges.

When BTK murdered victim No. 10—Dolores Davis— on January 19, 1991, I was staying once again with my parents in Park City, right after returning to Kansas from my California assignment for Pinkerton. The murder occurred 14 days before my 31st birthday.

After Mom had decoded *Project Broadway* she said, "I almost lost two daughters." She was confirming her belief that I almost became BTK's eleventh murder victim; also, that my sister Kim [13 years younger] had possibly been only moments from death.

That event happened in 1992. It terrified Mom.

Kim and her best friend Angie had been shopping for prom dresses at the Bride shop near closing time. The door had already been locked while Kim and Angie completed their shopping. Two lady clerks opened the door when they were ready to leave. A man appeared and held the door open until they had left. He quickly went inside, closing the door behind him.

Kim and Angie thought nothing of it.

The next day's news revealed the murders of the two clerks. It was suspected that the man was the I-70 Killer.

Twenty: The final confession

By the time the prosecution got to the Dolores Davis case on the second day of Dennis Rader's sentencing hearing, I felt like my body and emotions had been pulled through a tiny knothole backwards.

I couldn't sleep the night before. Whether my eyes were shut or open, I kept replaying in my mind over and over all the things that Dennis had said and done that now scared the crap out of me.

Sometimes it seemed as if the thoughts lingered like my brain was functioning in slow motion. Other times my thoughts overwhelmed me, rushing at me, as if unstoppable.

Project Broadwater ran across the ceiling like a never-ending banner. I thought of all the physical symptoms I'd shown that are similar to those caused by a certain date rape drug—and how I believed Dennis had been gradually poisoning me in an effort to get me to quit my job so that he could strangle me. I thought about all the weird, terrifying things that happened in the duplex apartment I lived in during the last few weeks before his arrest.

I thought about how the symptoms and the weird things all stopped the day Dennis was arrested, never to happen again. The nightmares, though, they had dug in, and would not go away.

I tried drinking myself to sleep. That didn't work. It just made my thoughts morph into more terrifying thoughts. I wanted to sleep. I was afraid to sleep, fearing the nightmares would be even more terrifying.

Anger at Dennis . . . anger at City Hall...anger at all the people who didn't believe me and believed Dennis instead . . . anger kept me going through the second day of testimony.

Only when I saw Gordon Wegerle, Charlie Otero, and Kevin Bright on the TV screen—saw the pain in their faces—did the anger abate. Though their pain was far the greater, I identified with them. They would know how and why I felt the way I did. They'd been there and been there and been there.

Any time I'd hear anyone say, "I know how you feel," I wanted to puke. I didn't always verbalize it, but I always thought it. *The hell you do! You go through what they did, then you can tell me you know how they feel . . . or how I feel.*

The surviving members of the victims' families that attended the sentencing hearing got the satisfaction of seeing Dennis Rader put away for 175 years in an 8 by 10-foot room. That didn't bring their loved ones back, but it was something, a silver bullet to the heart of evil. It didn't give me back six-and-one-half years of my life. But it was something. A relief in knowing that son-of-a-bitch will rot in prison. I hope his thoughts turn inward on him; morph into cancerous, never-ending nightmares, and that he sees over and over what he did to his victims will happen to him.

He will never again be able to do to anyone else what he did to Dolores Davis. The tenth and final person that Dennis confessed to torturing and murdering, she was 63 when he killed her on January 19, 1991.

She was a cat person. Once when I was prowling [at night], checking the phone line, a cat smacked the window. It was me out there casing the place.

I used the scout thing on that, too . . . Trappers Rendezvous . . . It's up at Harvey County Park West. It's a big thing for the scouts. They go up there in the dead of winter and camp out. Like the old trappers.

So that was my alibi and my cover. I went up there, set up camp, got it all set up. I fabricated some story like I had to go to town or back home for something.

I drove from there to my folks' house. I dressed in my hit kit, my hit clothes, at my folks' house.

I drove over to the Baptist church there in Park City. I had a key to that because that's where the scouts hung out. I went in there and did my final preparation for my walk. I walked into Davis' [place] from there. I basically went down across the street there at 61st, walked back behind...I could see through the window blinds that she was reading. Pretty soon the lights went out then I waited a while until I knew she was asleep, in case she heard me banging around.

[When] I broke the window she comes running out of her bedroom...she says, "What happened to my house? Did you hit my house?"

She thought a car had come through her house. [He'd thrown a cinder block through a sliding glass door.]

I said, "I'm wanted, they are after me. I need your house and your car and your money...eventually I'm going to tie you up and I'm going to leave you."

She kind of backed up. She said, "You can't be in the house."

I said, "Ma'am, you're going to cooperate. I've got a club, I've got a gun, I've got a knife...I suggest you do. You take your choice how you want it."

And she said, "Okay, okay."

That's the control factor. You start to control them a little bit; you ease them a little bit. Just like you guys, come in here and you buddy me, you try to make me feel at ease like it's going to be okay.

I really wanted to spend some time with her; but damn it, she said, "There's somebody coming."

I could not believe my luck in these places. I always got somebody coming.

I had already asked her where her keys were to her car, so I had those...that was one of my other things, to make sure I had a way to get out of there or a way to transport the person. I need to get her out of here. And the best way to get her out of here is go ahead and just put her down, yank her out of here.

She said, "You're not going to kill me? I got kids."

Too late, she told me she had kids, you know, "Don't hurt me."

I proceeded to tie her up and then I think she realized that this was going to go bad, and she said, "Don't kill me, don't kill me."

I slipped the pantyhose over her head and strangled her . . . two, three minutes . . . that was it with her. I just reached in the drawer and grabbed them . . . she still had some that stuff on her . . . she still had her house robe, when I strangled her, and I didn't take any pictures in the house because I thought, *This guy is coming.*

I put her on a bedspread and drug [sic] her through the house . . . and used that bedspread as leverage.

I was trying to find a place to hide her. I had to get back to the camp, I had a time constraints [sic]. I took her actually . . . I actually took her, dropped her down to the KDOT [Kansas Department of Transportation] . . . dropped her back in the bushes . . . it was snowing . . . it was cold.

[He got his own vehicle] . . . drove back to the KDOT lakes, loaded her up. And then I proceeded north. I was looking for that...really for a barn but the time frame, the strain and everything. I found this bridge and parked there and yanked her out and put her underneath the bridge.

My original plan was I was going to drop her under the bridge and come back the next night and take her to that barn and run her through the bondage pictures. But the next night was even worse, it was foggy, you couldn't see diddly squat on that night.

I took pictures the second night—if you find the pictures, I think you'll find where the animals had attacked her.

[He'd left a mask behind with the body.]

Painted it flesh tone color, lipstick, added eyebrows...I did that because it kind of prettied her up. More of a feminine type. That's my mask. I wear that mask, too. Pose myself in bondage pictures with this mask.

See, I painted it a flesh color, yes, nice lips and a little bit of a smile, like a pretty girl . . . and I would wear that when I would do my sexual fantasy things, my self bondage things. I would wear that. And I would try to take pictures so I looked like maybe I was a female or a person in distress.

Dolores Davis was Project Dogside—a portmanteau merger of the Hillside Road and the dog kennel near her property. His thinking in coming up with that code name, I believe, is identical to his thought process in coming up with the code name *Project Broadwater.* The duplex apartment I lived in when Dennis was arrested was located right off Broadway. A lagoon was right behind the duplex.

Still terrifies me.

Dennis Rader is a control freak, and the day that they hired me was Christmas morning and his best birthday present all wrapped into one. You see, until they hired me, the Compliance Department was a one-person deal, and Dennis had held the position seven years by himself.

Well, imagine being Dennis, and not only did they hire another officer to work in the Compliance Department, but they put the icing on the cake when they promoted him to supervisor at the same time. So here we are just a two-person department with King Shit, and a female employee working for him, that has to do what he says.

It was as if Dennis had a multitude of masks that he could change rapidly; the one he wore for his family, and others in the office, and the ones that he used to keep me in my place, beneath him and terrified.

After finding out so much about Dennis since his arrest, I would have to say, as did my psychologist, that the part of Dennis that required control as well as the part that bolstered his self-importance, was fulfilled the moment I was hired, and the City promoted him to supervisor.

Twenty-one: Park City hires me

It was during my marriage to Robert Campbell (1992-2002), that I first met Dennis Rader. I believe it was in 1997. My German shepherd, Jerry Lee, bit a neighbor's child. I called in the report, and stayed home from work so that when the Animal Control officer, Dennis Rader, showed up, I could show him all of Jerry Lee's paperwork.

He showed up just before lunch time. I invited him in, and gave him my verbal report as to what happened, and showed him the paperwork.

As I recall, when I invited Dennis in I also invited him to have a seat, which he did, and he took notes as well as the information from my driver's license. He was very polite and explained the situation to me, what would happen if the child's parents chose to file charges.

They didn't file charges, so I did not receive a citation.

Dennis was wearing a uniform, and had driven over in a City-marked vehicle. He gave me his business card when I first opened the door.

The only thing that bothered me at the time was that I had called in at 8:00 a.m., and it was almost four hours later before he showed up, and our house was only a block from City Hall.

Eight years later, after I knew Dennis' big secret, the thought that I'd actually invited this monster into my home repulsed me and scared the living crap out of me. I couldn't even hold a glass of Diet Pepsi for over a half-hour, my hands were shaking so. Nor could I hold a lighter steady enough to light up a cigarette.

There I was, addicted to Diet Pepsi and nicotine, and was so nervous for a while I couldn't even indulge in my habits.

But I didn't know the real Dennis in 1997, which is why I applied for the position of compliance officer for

Park City in July 1998. I was interviewed by a committee of Dee Stuart, city council member; Jack Whitson, Director of Economic Planning and Development; and Dennis Rader, recently promoted to Compliance Supervisor.

Jack and Dee focused on my past employment and job duties. Dennis asked only about my computer experience. I assured him that I indeed had Microsoft Word and Excel knowledge.

Whitson called that evening to offer the job. An official letter of job offer was then sent, and I accepted. On August 4, 1998 I began working for Park City under the supervision of Dennis Rader.

My training entailed two weeks of shadowing Dennis, both in the office and in the field. Right off, the coldness of his beady dead eyes etched an unforgettable image in my brain. I'd never seen eyes like that before. I did not like him—not that first day, nor the second, or any day, week, month, or year thereafter.

I made up my mind to not let my first impressions keep me from doing my job.

Dennis was initially concerned that City Hall would play favorites with me because my dad was the Police Chief; also, because my husband Robert was on the city council. That should have been the least of his concerns, as Dad bent over backward to avoid even the appearance of showing nepotism, and my husband distanced himself from any outward apparent interest in what I did on the job.

The position of compliance officer wasn't really that complex; however, due to the duties I would be involved in, I was required to be fingerprinted, and a triple I (the most thorough background check) was run on me. The city clerk then swore me in.

Dennis took me to Bay Singers, a local police uniform company, to buy equipment. He stressed the importance that we have raincoats, but the selection was limited to POLICE, FIRE and SECURITY silk-screened designnations. Instead of having them ordered, Dennis chose POLICE—this was written on the back in large black letters.

I pointed out that we were *compliance* officers, not *police* officers, and that people might think we were trying to impersonate police officers.

Dennis disagreed.

A tiny red flag began waving way in the deep recesses of my mind, but I ignored it. However, I held my ground and never wore the raincoat Dennis picked out for me, eventually getting a plain yellow rain slicker, which I felt was much more citizen friendly and not in any way intimidating.

It was during that training time that Dennis indicated that when he started there was no uniform, and that he'd picked out the color and style of the uniform: tan shirts, brown slacks, with a brown jacket, and brown ties, and, of course, a badge.

I couldn't count the times that citizens thought I was a Wichita police officer.

When the Park City police chief heard about the rain slicker with the word POLICE on the back, he stormed into our little compliance office and told Dennis in no uncertain terms that it would not be allowed, that Dennis was not a police officer, and he did not have the power to arrest people.

Dennis' face reddened and he said, "Fine! Just get me a new one and put dogcatcher on the back of it!"

His own designation as *dogcatcher* has come back to anger and haunt him many times. It is one of my favorite ways of thinking of him: ole dogcatcher.

Knowing how much Dennis really disliked being called *dogcatcher* is exactly why my publisher registered the domain name www.btkdogcatcher.com for the Internet marketing web site for this book.

A few years later, I would think it ironic that just as BTK was reemerging with his BTK Grams, that our uniforms were changed. Dennis was totally against the idea. I thought, as compliance officers, the new look was appropriate, not looking anything like the Wichita Police Department.

Dennis sarcastically termed our new duds:

Wildlife and Game.

He would at times continue to wear his brown uniform on what he called his "in field days," when he'd be out of the office and interacting with the community.

I was happy with the new uniform, which also was far more functional, and I never wore the other uniform again. One day Dennis lamented that, "I commanded respect and authority with the old uniform."

It wasn't until after his arrest that the full impact of that statement became crystal clear. He loved to control people, especially his murder victims. I think he felt a measure of control slip through his fingers when he was not allowed to look like a police officer.

Those first two weeks learning on the job were interesting.

Dennis began day one showing how he started every day; beginning with opening the compliance office, booting up the computer, unlocking file cabinets, and starting the paperwork.

Then we went into the field. At first I thought Dennis was good at training because he certainly was thorough. He was patient during that time, as well as polite except for his repetitive negative comments:

"You will not make friends in this job. You will be hated by most citizens; I know from experience," he would say.

I thought, *Maybe it's your approach that causes people to dislike you.*

Several things occurred during the two weeks' training that also raised flags in my mind.

Dennis had commented that he'd worked at ADT [the security alarm company], and was fired after over twelve years of service. His tone betrayed intense bitterness. He told me, "You never know when an employer will do it to you again."

I could almost see the big chip on his shoulder.

One day during a routine patrol with Dennis, we traveled down a street called Primrose where we encountered a dog running loose. Shadow was the dog's name. Dennis said the dog was a continuing problem. We finally got the dog back into the fenced-in area where it belonged.

A week or two later the dog was out again, and we tried to capture the dog. The owners were not home, and we eventually had to dart the dog due to its aggressive behavior and complaints from the neighbors. After Dennis darted the dog, it got away from us, and we were unable to find it. I was patrolling the area looking for the dog while Dennis returned to the owners' house.

Later that day I was told by the Chief of Police [my father] that the son of the property owner had arrived while Dennis was there, and this gentleman was an attorney, and he insisted that Dennis get off the property. Dennis refused and the gentleman indicated that he would file charges of trespassing, and this conversation was conducted in front of my father, who made sure that Dennis complied with the citizen's request.

Dennis was not happy about this turn of events. Citations were served later in the week to the property owners.

When Dennis was arrested for the murders of ten people, the attorney that represented the owners was interviewed. He pointed out the unbelievable amount of paperwork that Dennis presented in the case, as well as the codes he used for everything. The owners had been found guilty.

I believe the owners would not have taken it as far as they did, except they were dealing with Dennis Rader. He got under their skin with his arrogant attitude that he was a compliance officer, and that entitled him by city ordinance to enter any yard he deemed necessary, whether or not he was asked to leave because of trespassing, even if—in his mind—the action violated a person's 4th Amendment rights.

But, no, Dennis wanted to make sure with his attitude that he commanded respect.

In most instances, though, what it likely commanded was citizen fear or anger, rather than respect.

Another time, Dennis was serving a citation to a citizen for failure to comply with the City Health & Safety Ordinance regarding inoperable vehicles. He parked in front of the house on the opposite side of the street, stepped out of the vehicle and took pictures of the subject car, and then got back into the compliance vehicle, all while I remained in the passenger seat.

Dennis began filling out a citation, which he called "our bread and butter tickets."

I asked why, and he replied that we had two different citations: one that we could fill out on the spot; and the other was more formal, and was typed.

While Dennis was bent forward filling out the citation, I noticed that a man walked out of the house and was proceeding toward us. I indicated this to Dennis, and he never even looked up; he just asked me in a hateful tone of voice, "Are you scared...are you sure you can do this job as a woman?"

I felt insulted, and replied that I wasn't afraid, just making him aware that someone was approaching the vehicle.

Dennis' attitude toward that gentleman was total arrogance. I felt embarrassed for the man, for the demeaning way that Dennis spoke to him.

The last thing I felt worth noting about my two weeks' training happened on a hot August afternoon. We received a call from a trailer park that a woman was outside her front door beating her cat.

We went to the location, and Dennis was able to get the cat from the woman. We took it to the local vet. The cat was panting very hard, and had blood all over it and was obviously in shock. The woman apparently had been beating the cat as well as swinging it so that it hit the house, as well as the deck on the house.

The cat didn't make it.

We went back to the house to take a report only to find that the woman had removed all of her furniture, and put it in the dumpster. We knocked on the door, and the women invited us in, which was too hot to be in. She didn't have the central air on; however, she did have the heater on.

Asked why she was abusing her cat, she replied that the cat was possessed by Satan, as was her furniture, and that's why she had the heater on—to run off the evil.

Dennis tried to find out who her relatives were, but she was not forthcoming with that information. He asked if he could call her pastor or anyone so they could come help her.

"No," was her terse, very terse, reply

We left, but Dennis continued making contacts until he found her father, who did call an ambulance later that evening.

After Dennis' arrest, I searched my mind and could only remember this and one other time that I had personally witnessed my boss showing compassion for another human being. The other occasion was in 2001.

While Dennis was on patrol, he came across a young boy about five or six who appeared to be lost. He made contact with the child, and remained with him while he contacted the police department on the radio. It was very cold outside, so Dennis also told the police that he was putting the child in his vehicle.

The child had gotten on the wrong bus and ended up in Park City. The police located the mother, and reunited her with her son. The next day the mother showed up with baked cookies for Dennis as a thank you.

I've often revisited in my mind the job interview with Jack Whitson, Dee Stuart and Dennis Rader. I was sitting in the middle in front of Jack's desk, facing Jack. Dee sat in front, but close enough to lay her notes down on top of Jack's desk.

Jack was reared back in his chair in a very relaxed position. Dee also was very relaxed and comfortable.

Dennis was neither.

He sat square in his chair with his legs and feet clenched together, some papers sitting on his knees. He constantly looked down at the papers, as Jack and Dee did most of the talking.

His posture was not professional.

When I was hired to work in the Compliance Department my father was the Chief of Police. We worked in completely different departments for the same city— that's where the association ended.

I was told by both Jack Whitson and my dad that I would not receive special privileges because of my father. I said that I didn't want any favors, as I only wanted to be considered on my own merits.

Jack separately informed me that Dennis was very concerned about the fact he'd be supervising the Chief's daughter, and was worried the Chief would get involved because of Dennis's style of supervision.

Twenty-two: Playing his game

After the two weeks of training, Dennis told Jack that I was picking up on the job fairly well and could start working on my own. That was perfectly fine with me as I already felt I needed a break from the routine of all-day contact with Dennis. I've always been a quick study and self-motivated. I was determined to show City Hall that they'd made not a good hire, but an outstanding hire.

Right after I was hired, Dennis was curious about my past employment with Pinkerton's Security & Investigations, especially after learning that I'd left as manager for the Kansas Office. He'd ask questions as if he was thinking out loud. But it always seemed to piss him off when I'd respond about the duties I was responsible for. I learned quickly that Dennis needed his ego boosted, and no way could I appear to be smarter than him, or know more.

Multiple times he said, "You cannot know more than me. I'm the supervisor."

So to keep the peace I played his game, and would play up to that huge ego of his. For example, I placed a note on top of my files that said, FOR YOUR REVIEW AND APPROVAL

He loved that one.

Or even if I knew the answer, I'd ask for advice about a case that I might be working on. He enjoyed that as well because it gave him the opportunity to show that, well—in his mind—he was smarter than me.

Sometimes this game helped keep him in a good mood. I tried not to bring up to him knowledge about anything that might undermine his opinion except on occasions I felt it was absolutely necessary, and there were many such occasions.

I was efficient on my patrols, always giving verbal warnings the first time and citations on the second offense; writing a lot of citations; also, issuing a lot of Health & Safety Violation letters regarding inoperable vehicles.

Often I was getting complimented on what a good job I was doing from citizens, and other city employees. This did not sit well with Dennis, and that is when the nit-picking began. It never stopped, Dennis only getting more and more hateful and condescending all during the years I worked for Park City.

Those first few months I pretty much kept my feelings to myself about what a total ass Dennis was. I noticed that Jack, our boss, and several of the City Council members knew Dennis from the Boy Scout days, and at times, it seemed, pretty chummy. It became quite obvious to me early on that it was a Good ole boy back-slapping network, and my complaints—when I started making them—were chalked up to me being a female with mood swings from that time of the month. Because Dennis, although a certified jerk, they apparently figured he wasn't doing anything wrong.

Looking back on all that happened, I'm just plain pissed that I worked for probably the most narrow-minded, ignorant people on the planet.

Sure, it's my opinion, and I'm entitled to it. By God, I earned this right the hard way, showing up for work all those years, looking into the eyes of evil, while doing my job trying to keep my own sanity intact.

Those people wanted to play with the big dogs, but they couldn't manage to get off the front porch and put down their coffee mugs to get an education on the legal system to protect their employees and the citizens of Park City. Because if they had, Dennis would never have been enabled by this same group of government leaders to have even been promoted, let alone allow me to endure six years of pure hell.

I'd wake up every morning thinking *this is the DAY!* Today one of the Powers That Be will see Dennis' shit for what it is, and I will be set free. But hell no. Even when *both* the Police Department of Wichita and the FBI showed up to serve the warrant on the City of Park City for a search, what do you think came from their stupid ignorant mouths?

"If you're here to arrest Dennis on anything Mary Capps said, she's crazy."

So now I was *really* pissed off, because here we have the FBI and the Chief of Police for the City of Wichita standing there serving them a warrant—and they are still standing by the son-of-a-bitch. Can you really freaking believe it? Idiots—they called me crazy!

I'm pissed off because I don't know when I will ever gain the trust that I will need to ever find employment. Because after six years of this shit, my mind has been so brain washed to believe that I'll never find an employer who will listen to me if or when I have a problem with a fellow employee.

I'm pissed that because of their attitude, I started questioning my own sanity. I'm pissed because they never asked how I was doing after Dennis was arrested and confessed. They never even gave me an explanation as to why I was sent home the day he was arrested: just that they were complying with a Federal investigation, and they wouldn't answer the question if I was the one being investigated.

You know, a couple months after Dennis was arrested I realized that I wasn't just his next victim. I already was a victim that the city had given him as a toy, for his personal amusement, and his hateful, evil side, with his control, harassment, bullying, and abuse.

The bottom line is that the city empowered him with that promotion to be the dick that he was.

No, I wasn't murdered, but I sure in hell am a surviving victim.

I got so depressed at one point that I wanted to know what was wrong with me, that I couldn't function outside my own little world—where I lived behind a six-foot fence with the gate padlocked at all times. I feared to go out in public at times, yet Dennis' wife returned back to work soon after, and moved freely throughout this same city, shopping, working, as if it never happened.

So here is the question I asked myself over and over: *Am I crazy, or is it the rest of the world?*

Thank God, that with counseling and the support of my family and now with the love of a really good man, I've regained my life. My family call me Mary Nova. Nova is my middle name. Well, I want you to know that Mary Nova is back.

But, yes, it still hurts like hell to go back and relive what I went through because of Dennis Raider—but if I don't do it, you will never hear all of my side of the story. What you do with the revelations in this book—that is up to you.

Anyway, Dennis started nitpicking everything I did. One day he would look at my Notice of Violation letters then tell me to include the middle initial in my signature. The next day, he wouldn't like the position of my officer number, and would tell me to redo the letters.

I began to feel that if he couldn't find a mistake, he would make one up. It became uncomfortable to be in the same room with him. He might open a filing cabinet, but upon closing it he would slam it, which I never knew when it was coming. So it always startled me, making me jump and causing my stomach to knot.

We had contrasting work habits. Dennis was very slow; I worked quickly. This is why for every Notice of

Violation that he put out, I put out three and was still able to have all my paperwork down and filed the next morning before patrol.

I began complaining—to Jack, to Carol, as well as other employees—about the treatment I was receiving from Dennis. But my boss was a master of disguise and, although other employees didn't or wouldn't work for Dennis, they did not see the side that I saw of Dennis; simply, they didn't want to get involved. He made sure that nobody saw or heard what he was doing to me.

I filed the first grievance with Mayor Olin Heibert. (He'd been both Dennis' and my high school English teacher, although a number of years apart.) Jack told me, "Mary, you can't do it this way. You have to file it with your immediate supervisor."

"What?" I said in astonishment. "The grievance IS about my immediate supervisor. How can—"

Jack cut me off. "It's in the Personnel Manuel."

"Like I was trying to say, how could Dennis properly and objectively investigate the grievance regarding his actions toward me?"

"It's policy," Jack said. "You have to follow policy."

I felt like I was talking to a brick wall.

No, I take that back. I might have had more success with a brick wall than I did complaining to some of the people in our city government.

Dennis was a lot larger than I was, maybe 195 pounds or so and close to six-feet. When I was hired to work for Park City, I weighed about 160 pounds, mostly muscle packed on my just-under 5-4 frame. I wore a size 12. You might say that I was pretty fit. I could lift a heavy steel cage containing a 50-pound dog and load it in the back of my truck.

Dennis also was pretty fit. He took a lot of walks during the nice weather with his dog "Dudley."

In December 2000 I started losing weight after my brother committed suicide, and by the next summer I was wearing a size 6. I stayed that size until after Dennis was arrested and then I started gaining weight.

Twenty-three: The summit conference

I followed Jack's order and filed my grievance with Dennis. And, sure enough, Dennis felt that his rights were violated. I don't know how he rationally came to that conclusion, but that is what he concluded. I was the one filing the grievance—not Dennis.

A few days later Dennis requested a meeting with me, saying that Carol Jones, our city clerk, would be in the room at the time for both our protection, since I was a female and the door to our office would be closed.

Well, the meeting took place in our tiny office: two desks and a little computer desk crammed into a space designed for one person. Our desks faced each other, with barely enough room to maneuver our desk chairs in between for the sit-down meeting. We sat facing each other.

Carol sat in the chair by the computer desk, scant feet from us. She is a large-boned—not fat—upper middle-aged lady who wears glasses and dresses business; nice clothes but her flat shoes and long hem length give her a kind of matronly look. She didn't say a word.

Dennis, holding the grievance papers, leaned forward. If I'd also leaned forward, we could've bumped each other—we were sitting that close.

He hesitated a moment then spoke. "Mary, you should have talked to me. That would have been better. If by anyway I have offended you, then I apologize."

I thought he was sincere. His voice was not threatening, not whining, but comfortable. What he said and did next both shocked and bothered me. The steadiness of his voice wavered as he revealed, "There are so many compliments coming from everybody—that with your job performance, I'm concerned they will want to put the old horse out to pasture."

He started choking up with those last few words and started crying. He pulled a handkerchief out of a pocket and dabbed at his eyes. While he was doing that, I responded. "Dennis, I'm not trying to take your job. Every successful supervisor surrounds himself with hard-working employees who get their jobs done. You should look at that as a compliment reflecting on you."

Things did improve—for a while. Then Dennis began to systematically dispatch my dignity, while shredding my confidence, and whittling my self-esteem to a bloody stub.

You might call it practice for what he really wanted to do to me.

A lot was happening in my life during my tenure as an employee of Park City, Kansas.

My marriage with Councilman Robert Campbell flamed out, I was arrested for civil disturbance and my brother Jeff committed suicide.

I married Rod only to have that marriage annulled when my husband's best friend convinced him that I was crazy, and became engaged to Rod again when he realized that his "best friend" was just trying to get me out of Rod's life.

But, while you read of the above events in coming chapters, please keep in mind that I remain really good friends with Robert and Rod. They are good people. We just weren't made for each other, and people get hurt when you just try to ride it out. They are very active in my children's as well as my grandchildren's lives. They really do care for me and my family.

Twenty-four: His odd-ball quirks

Although Dennis had seemed quite sincere during our grievance meeting, he was not sincere enough to give me a job review that would have helped me establish a career. Rather, it was not bad and not really good, just sort of ho-hum; actually, the kind of review designed for a supervisor to keep his job—definitely not to reward me in any way.

For a time things appeared to be normal, but then Dennis found new ways to pick, as well as use facial expressions in efforts to intimidate me. To me, it wasn't what he said as much as his body language and the facial expressions that were most upsetting.

Then one day Dennis' anger ratcheted up several notches.

I was returning from the animal shelter where I'd taken an animal, when I came across a woman whose car had broken down on the road. I stopped and offered help, remaining with her until she was able to start her vehicle.

When I got back to City Hall and walked into the office, Dennis grabbed the notebook from my hands, screaming at me to tell him where I'd been. My attempts at answering were drowned out by his continued hysterics, and stabbing his finger at my ride log.

"Where were you? Ten minutes there, 20 minutes at the shelter, ten minutes back? Answer me! Can't you think?"

The entire time he was glaring at me.

I never got to give him an answer, because he didn't want one. He just wanted to beat me down. I just stood there shaking while he chewed me out.

I found out later that Dennis had been trying to radio me on the city radio that was in my vehicle, but I was out of the vehicle at the time of his calls. What it all boiled down to was that an animal control call had come in, and Dennis didn't want to leave the office; he wanted me to hurry back from the shelter and take the call. He was just plain pissed off that he had to respond himself. As I've said: Dennis really hated the dogcatcher role and designation. Tee-hee.

Dennis Rader was the C o m p l i a n c e S u p e r v i s o r, and he loved that title. He loved wearing a uniform. And he loved sitting in front of people's houses taking his sweet ass time, writing things on a note pad, which he held high enough in the air so that anyone inside of their home was sure to see.

Did I believe this caused anxiety for those people?

You bet I did, particularly since it might take him up to six months or longer to do anything with what he might have documented as a violation. Those poor unsuspecting citizens never knew when Dennis was going to send them a notice. He just sat back and enjoyed the misery he created. It was a side of himself he revealed during his sentencing hearing.

I never understood at the time why Dennis would document so much stuff, and then just sit on it for months and months. It only involved inoperable vehicles, miscellaneous clutter in a yard, or perhaps a house that badly needed painted—nothing like a felony crime you'd want to build a case on. He obviously was performing high drama in those instances, learning where the pauses and rhythms belonged, where they produced the most anxiety and pain. Like tying up a little naked girl and women and watching them die. Slowly and in pain. For him, such anxiety and excruciation merely was the stuff of masturbation and release for himself.

I, on the other hand, would also track items, but always got to them within a few weeks, vehicles within 30 days, and only that long because the City Ordinance required vehicles to be tracked for 30 days.

One of Dennis' favorite sayings was, "They're not Better Homes and Garden people." I'd even heard him say that to citizens about other citizens.

I could not—even months after his arrest—believe that Park City's management felt that Dennis had done any wrong: he was just being Dennis; although odd, he was doing a good job; and the entire time he's giving citizens in the city ulcers.

He would even refer to people at City Hall as *attitude-y*—although not a word, that's what he used, and directed it at them.

I held out hope right up to the very day of his arrest that someday someone was going to wake up and see what I saw in Dennis—a mean, spiteful, manipulative, arrogant SOB, who not only harassed me, but the citizens of Park City

Who did he choose most often to pick on?

Well, it was the ones that were less fortunate; the ones that might need a little help; maybe it might be an extension of time to be in compliance. Whatever their need might be, it certainly didn't mean that they were bad people—on the contrary, they were hard-working citizens, honest, and trying to raise families.

But it was easy for Dennis to manipulate this as well, because if a complaint was called in on Dennis, who were they going to believe—the person with the violations and run-down yard, or Dennis?

I don't believe that Dennis—despite being a lay leader in his church and involved with the Cub Scouts—ever got the biblical concept of *Treat others as you would like to be treated.*

I believed that with the correct attitude the results were ultimately what the city was looking for. Of course, there were indeed times we were taken advantage of by citizens; but for the majority, they just needed a reminder, direction, and kind words.

As far as showing up early for work and leaving late, and his many quirks, Dennis functioned very predictively.

He always had a large bottle of hand lotion on his desk, and he used it all the time. He told me that he liked to keep his hands soft, and that during the winter he didn't like the rough feeling. The thing is there really wasn't anything too odd about this except that I always measured men against my father, who would never have a bottle of hand lotion on his desk. Most men I knew that used skin lubricants or conditioners during the winter months usually used Corn Huskers.

Dennis always wore a ball cap in the field, and when he came in, would comb his hair as soon as taking off his hat. He didn't have much hair on top, but he still combed it. On cold days he would wear a ball cap with ear mufflers over that and a scarf around his neck, which he would pull up to cover his mouth. He was picky about his hair and would get a haircut twice a month.

He hated the smell of cigarette smoke. Having a very keen sense of smell, he could smell anything.

One year when Park City was taking all city employees to the Greyhound Park for a Christmas party, we were served a buffet-style meal. Dennis told me that whenever he ate buffet-style, he always used his left hand to dish his food using the public spoon, so that when he sat down to eat he used his right hand so as not to get germs.

Dennis belched all the time. He said it was because of acid-reflux.

While talking he'd often rub his fingers together or rub his forehead. He brought his break snacks in plastic containers and kept them locked in his desk, as well as bringing several different flavors of soft drinks to work. During the months before his arrest, he started drinking a lot of coffee.

He took his morning break and afternoon break, as well as his lunch break, at the same time every day. The last year he started walking around the building, stretching his arms during his afternoon break. He never left work before 5:30 p.m., and until the last year, he always was at work by 7:45 a.m., but the last year he was pushing 8:00 a.m.

Dennis used a lot of the same lingo over and over, such as "Odds and ends" and "Same O, Same O."

And when he was having one of his rare good days, he'd lower his voice and ever so slowly drag out a guttural "*O h   y e a h h h h h.*"

That creeped me out.

When our new office was built and Dennis had his very own private exit and entrance into City Hall, he brought in a rug so that when he entered he could wipe his feet. And next to the rug, he kept his pair of office slippers. He would at times take his work boots off and put on his slippers, or walk around in his socks.

He brought in plants and a lot of family pictures. There were photos of his wife, son, and daughter, as well as family pictures taken on fishing trips and a KU [Kansas University] game.

The last year he was there he and his wife Paula were working on their house and Dennis brought in a very large painting he said his daughter had painted when she was younger.

Dennis also kept newspapers, and would recycle them after he cut articles out of them which he did daily during his morning break. By the way, while he was on break he would turn his telephone on to *away* so that he could not be disturbed. If I didn't know he was on break, or anyone else for that matter, and another person or I tried to talk to him, he would very rudely remind the intruder that he was on his 15-minute break.

In short, Dennis Rader is all about Dennis Rader.

You want an example of how inflated Dennis Rader's ego is?

Well here it is.

One day in the year 2000, Dennis showed up at work with a professionally decorated cake adorned with an animal control officer with a dog on a leash. The wording on the cake said "Congratulations Dennis Rader for 500 Animal Control citations."

He placed the cake in the break room with colorful plates and napkins with a note that read "Enjoy."

I stood in the break room looking at this cake, along with some other employees, all of us laughing. One of the detectives left to get a camera to take a picture, because he was sure no one would believe him. He kidded that maybe he should have a cake made to celebrate how many speeding tickets he'd written.

Meanwhile, I was standing there smoking a Marlboro Light, with so many mixed emotions and thoughts running through my mind.

"Oh, BOY! Here it is—he's in trouble now; someone in Management or a Council member is going to see how unethical this is. What a freaking egotistical idiot!"

To my disappointment, nothing was said to him about the cake, except for maybe, "Thanks for bringing the cake; it was good."

I thought for sure that someone would see this cake for what it was—a representation of a harassing jerk. But I couldn't have been more surprised by their response than if he'd stood there in a clown costume holding the cake, and was passing out balloons to go along with it.

They just didn't get it.

They didn't want to see it, which would mean they'd have to deal with it, and there were more important things than really looking at what Dennis was doing. Even Dennis said the same thing during his interrogation: "The office, because Park City has a lot going on, is too busy to keep track of me."

Twenty-five: His "BTK codes"

The first several months—until I got my own computer—
Dennis and I shared one. He used the Excel program for
tracking some items, and he used the program Access to
track other things. For everything that was entered into
the Access program it had a code which Dennis designed.

For example:

AWCLR meant *awaiting certified letter.*

SHCKI *shelter check in.*

N *nuisance.*

NV *nuisance vehicle.*

He had hundreds of codes. All the entries were
coded. In Excel, he would do the same, except he would
put them in a file, then put that in a file, and then again in
another file. And every one of them had a code.

I could spend an entire afternoon trying to crack his
codes so I could find something. It frustrated me. You'd
think he was holding onto top secret information for the
CIA, and it was up to him to make sure that no one found
it, except on a *need-to-know* basis.

Little did I know what he really was hiding.

No one that worked at City Hall gave a hoot, or even
cared about our files, and what they might pertain to. I
believed that he surely knew—or at least should have
known—better than anyone else that no one was looking
at those files in the office on that computer. Besides,
what person guilty of ten murders would be so brazen as
to keep all the evidence in his office? Only someone with
a sick kind of confidence.

The city had much faith and trust in Dennis, and he
knew it. That was reflected in the fact that he got that
private office entrance in 2000—the mayor didn't even
have a private entrance.

So there was Dennis forcing his codes, what I later would call his "BTK codes," on me. During his interrogation after his arrest, the police asked about the codes that he used in his communications through the years. The officer said it was a German Fractional code that Dennis had learned in the Air Force. It gave the FBI analyst fits trying to make sense of it. Yet, I was expected—more times than I can remember—to be able to receive and understand written instructions from Dennis in code.

I got where I would just stare down at the piece of paper and feel something surge through me, leaving me shaking and thinking, *What in the world did I do wrong to be punished by years of working for such an idiot?*

Then I'd stare some more, wishing a code key would appear magically, which would prevent me from the need to go stand in front of Dennis and inquire as to the meaning, only to be berated for being a complete moron, and perhaps needing more training:

"What. . . . you can think? You're acting like a new hire, and should know this stuff after this long."

I'd leave the office after being educated and reminded of my complete lack of knowledge and made to understand what a privilege it was to work in the presence of such a genius. It didn't matter how many times or to whom I complained about the codes, because Dennis was always victorious and got his way. He'd give some bullshit excuse for the absolute necessity for the codes.

And they *always believed him.*

Every day he'd come up with new codes, because he always came up with a new form or a new way to hide the secrets to finding the Holy Grail, because that's what he must have believed he was holding onto. Only after his arrest did the rest of the world and I learn the contents of what he called *The mother lode.*

But the codes didn't start or end there. Also, there were case numbers. When I was hired, he kept the case numbers in a three-ring binder. Simple: when we cut a case we assigned a case number in logical sequence. Here's where it got interesting. I started in August of 1998, and from that date until December 1999 we shared case numbers, meaning that my case number could be the one following his.

My point was that anyone in any type of law enforcement knew that a trespassing case number could be followed by a homicide. But not with Dennis. If I sent out a violation notice for grass, it was a case number especially for grass; if it was for a dog running at large then it had a different set of case numbers specially designed by Dennis Rader, and so on.

But starting with January 1999 this stayed the same except for citation case numbers—those case numbers were designed for items that required the violator to appear in court. One day when I arrived at work, Dennis said he'd set up a set of case numbers for me, and a set for himself, for citations. Here's how it worked:

Say, for example, I wrote a citation for *animal running at large,* my case number might be ACC99-1-10C; his might be ACC00-1-300R. The ACC stood for Animal Control Citation, the 99 for the year. The *1* was for how many so far to date for the year of 99, and *10* for how many I had written since employed, and the C for my last name.

I believe his only reason for doing this was so that he could count the notches on his belt. In other words, he had, inadvertently or otherwise, devised the perfect system to demonstrate what an excellent dogcatcher he really was.

But I couldn't believe my ears—what he told his boss. He told Jack it was so he could keep track of my work.

PLEASE!!!

Did Dennis Rader steal my dreams?

You bet he did.

Because of him, City Hall never got the chance to see what a truly wonderful employee I was, because it was all filtered through Dennis. I have always worked hard at every job that I've had; and worked my way up, but I didn't get the chance to do that while an employee of Park City.

Twenty-six: Pushing buttons

Those first few years working for Park City, I never had a problem standing my ground with Dennis. Jack Whitson would even tell me to give it back to him, and I wasn't one for holding back. I had spunk, and never could be accused of being a coward or soft spoken.

I would later recall occasions that sent shivers up my spine—times when I probably came real close to pushing buttons that might've sent my boss over the edge.

One time Dennis called me into his office area, and told me to have a seat. By the look on his face I knew he was pissed, but I was in no mood to take any of his crap. Earlier that day Dennis had sent me out on a loose cattle call, and he stayed in the office. He told me before I left on the call to not bother him because he was getting ready for lunch.

So I went to the location where the cattle were loose, and one hour later and a horn-honking traffic jam, the police and I were able to get the cattle back to their owner.

After the mess was over, the Police Chief asked me, "Who the hell does Dennis think he is, tying up the entire Police Department doing his job while he sits there soaking up the air conditioning?"

I said, "What the hell am I supposed to do? I'm the employee; Dennis is the boss."

Then I went to lunch. Dennis summoned me when I returned. Right off, he started screaming at me. "Why didn't you tell me the Chief was pissed? He went over my head to Jack!"

I replied. "It's not my place to tell you who's pissed off and who isn't."

"It certainly is!" he stormed. His eyes were bugged and glared his anger—his outraged anger.

I got up to leave. "Sit back down!" he yelled.

"I'm not going to have this conversation with you," I responded.

He kept yelling, "I TOLD YOU TO SIT DOWN!"

It felt like my heart beats were thundering. I could feel my face turning red. I stuck my fingers in my ears and yelled back, "I CAN'T HEAR YOU. LOOK, I'M LEAVING!"

I walked right out trembling in anger, and got in my truck and went on patrol.

In my mind, to say that Dennis had compassion for other people would be like saying the Pope doesn't like to attend mass: totally not in his character.

Late in 1999, I awoke one morning to find that someone had dismantled my van, and every window was bashed out, as well as the taillights, headlights, and parts were strewn up and down the street. I called work to say that I'd be late because I had to clean up the mess—didn't want Dennis himself catching me out of compliance—and wait for the police so I could file a report.

What was Dennis' reply?

"Sounds like a personal problem."

The year 2000 was more of the same. I told my husband what was going on, but Robert was still a City Council member and said he could not get involved.

Then a tragic event happened December 3rd that year which deeply impacted me—my younger brother Jeff committed suicide.

It was a Sunday, and I was at the Senior Center helping prepare for Park City's 25th anniversary, and there was a reception planned. I was helping with balloons when my other brother Hobert came into the common room where I was with the mayor and several council members. I knew by the look on my brother's face that something bad had happened. He told me to come to him, and he gathered me into a tight embrace, and then told me the worst news of my life. We dropped to the floor together, crying.

My parents were distraught, and I—being the oldest of four surviving children—felt I had to be strong for everyone. I went through the motions, not sleeping for several days; I couldn't sleep as I kept having visions of my dead brother, who had no enemies and knew no stranger.

City Hall closed out of respect for Jeff's father, the Police Chief. Everyone attended the funeral—except for Dennis. Two months previous, my grandmother had passed away, and now—the day before Jeff's funeral— Dennis said to me, "You're coming back to work as soon as the service is over, aren't you?"

I couldn't believe how uncaring he was. I didn't go back to work, staying instead with my family, as I should have.

The week after Jeff's passing, I went back to work, but it was Christmas time, and everyone was in a joyful mood. But with the wishes for the Season, and the non-ending questions about how my family and I were doing, I thought I was going to crack. I went to the doctor—he took me off work until after Christmas.

Two months later, one of my uncles died. This time I went to work before and after the service as I'd used up all my vacation time following Jeff's death. I knew that Dennis had no empathy for the things that can't be controlled but by God.

His reply was always, "It sounds like a personal problem."

One time Dennis and I were really going at it over his statement that I was spending too much time in the field. I was p-i-s-s-e-d. Jack came in and stood between us. I leaned around Jack and told Dennis, "I stay in the field because I can't stand to be in the same room with you."

That must've really ticked Dennis, because he replied, "Jack, did you hear that? She said she couldn't stand to be around me."

I considered it a well-deserved punch to his ego. And I'd have given a week's pay to know what Jack *really* felt about my statement.

You know, looking back, I don't think Jack Whitson gave a hoot if Dennis and I decided to put on the gloves and go at it—as long as it didn't interfere with his already busy schedule. I believe that cavalier attitude enabled Dennis to go about his daily clipping of items from the paper and magazines, secure in the knowledge that he had carte blanch approval to do whatever he damned well pleased on Park City's time.

Jack was always in a hurry, wheeling and dealing. His pat responses were:

"I don't have time for this."

"I'm telling you, it's not a big deal."

"Don't have time; can't talk about it now."

What employer would turn loose an employee and allow him to do all the supply ordering, uniform ordering, allow him to use the city vehicle for personal use to and from work and for lunch, allow him to sit in his office and create the "form of the day", and to top it all off—give him the ability and enable him to be Hitler to his only subordinate—if he did give a hoot?

Oh, I forgot, and give him his own private entrance—unless it was for no other reason than *I don't want to be bothered with this department because I have bigger fish to catch*—and yet never follow up to ensure that there weren't any problems.

I had not consumed alcohol for quite some time before working for Park City. But after just a few months into my association with Dennis Rader, I was drinking beer nightly to untie the knots in my stomach so I could go to sleep.

My smoking habit accelerated.

I'd always have a pack of Marlboro Lites with me, the short ones in a box. When I first opened a pack, I'd always take all of the plastic off the outside, and the foil on the inside top. I don't know why, but the plastic on the packs bugged me.

Twenty-seven: The Bob and Mary Show

I swear there were times my marriage to Robert Camp-bell resembled a soap opera. He was a good man: city councilman, good provider, good to my kids—but he had a side to him that I just could not become reconciled with.

We married in 1992 and were divorced in 2002—ten years that at times became more interesting than I felt they should have.

Let me explain.

I had left Bob the first time when I found out that he had a girlfriend in the Internet world. After a separation of about six months, he convinced me that he had changed and that he wouldn't do it again. However, in February 2002 I discovered that he was back at it again, only with a local person he met at a bar.

Bob liked to sing and would go to the local bar about a mile from our house to sing Karaoke. I've heard people say that he did a very good Elvis impersonation; in my opinion, maybe too good an impersonation.

I did not go. For one thing, I can't sing, and for another, I no longer cared for the bar scene. However, I would pop in for about 30 minutes once in awhile. Perhaps I should have dropped in more often. Even-tually, I became suspicious of one particular woman and her family. Bob told me that there was nothing going on between them.

To make a long story short, indeed, he and this woman had become *very* good friends, as I found out when I hacked into his PC and found their e-mails.

In March 2002, I had spent the evening with two friends—a couple—that lived across the street that also worked for Park City, in the Police Department. We had been drinking a few beers. About 11:00 p.m., I told them that I was tired, and that I was going home. After getting into bed, I paged Bob to tell him that I was home. His reply was that I was drunk, and he wasn't coming home. So I got dressed and went to the bar. When I arrived I was mad as hell, and the bar owner held me outside because I was yelling at the top of my lungs.

"Tell that lying, cheating, son-of-a-bitch to get his ass outside!"

Every one of the drunks said that I was mistaken, that nothing was going on between the two of them, and I was arrested and hauled off to jail. Oh, by the way, I'd also called this woman's husband, but she convinced him that I was nuts. Well, after going to jail, I decided that she could have him. Guess what. Although I was the crazy one, she moved in with Bob.

I spent the night in jail for doing nothing but telling the truth, clearly since they now lived together. I made a pact with myself that I'd never again allow a man to bullshit me.

When my court appearance came up, the city prosecutor met with me in private and told me my options—that if I pled not guilty they would bring in a different judge and prosecutor since I was an officer of the court and brought cases before these same two people. Well, I told Stan that I was guilty of yelling the exact wording of what was listed on the citation. So I took the informal diversion—the eight-hour anger management class. Then I divorced Bob and moved out with my son Kyle.

By that time, I dreaded going to the office, seeing Dennis' dead, beady eyes.

I lived for Saturday morning. Saturday was a FREE day. A day without Dennis—a day I could feel like a human being.

After I left Bob, Kyle and I moved into a little house on North Hydraulic. Kyle was 15 then. Come Saturday, I'd wake up early, throw on my robe, open the curtain to let in the sun's early rays, grab my morning Diet Pepsi, and dance my way over to the stereo, turn it up high and groove along with Tom Jones as he sang *What's new, Pussy Cat?*

Kyle didn't share his mom's enthusiasm for this early morning ritual. He'd come out of his room, a blanket wrapped around him, only one eye open, his spiked hair standing on end, and plod to the stereo to turn it off. Sometimes he didn't get out of bed, just groped from under his covers, out for his stereo, cranking up the driver for the kind of noise he and his peers called music.

I would just smile and enjoy the morning.

A day without Dennis was a slice of Heaven.

Every day upon arriving for work, I'd say, "Good morning," to Dennis, and he would respond—if he didn't then I knew he was already in a foul mood, and that would set my nerves on edge because I never knew what was coming. The last year we worked together it got worse. I'd be sitting at my desk working—which meant Dennis had to walk by to enter into the rest of the building; and it was as if I weren't there, and he didn't see me. It was like he had tunnel vision, and it was getting creepier by the day.

I guess being a serial murderer changes you. It was certainly changing *him.*

On such days I'd quickly get my ride log ready, and gather up what I needed in the field and then sneak out of the office so he wouldn't hear or see me leave.

At the time, I never analyzed why I did this, but after hours of sessions with a psychologist, I realized it was because I was afraid of him, subconsciously, because there'd been plenty of times I'd stood my ground with Dennis, and now my fear of him was increasing—frankly, it scared the hell out of me to be around him.

There was one day when I asked myself, *Does Paula actually wear the pants at home, instead of Dennis?*

Here's why.

Dennis had this older station wagon that he called his cruiser. It was gray or silver. He used it for his fishing and camping trips. Then Dennis bought his son's pickup. Paula told him that the station wagon had to go. It really upset him. I would later wonder if the wagon was the vehicle he'd used when he was active as BTK.

Through it all, my work attendance remained good— at least during those earlier years it was good. But I began having problems with my legs. It felt like my muscles were paralyzed, and I lost the use of my left leg. The muscles in my calf froze. I went to doctor after doctor, through test after test. Finally, one doctor diagnosed me with fibromyalgia. Three months with a leg brace, and I regained use of my leg.

But the symptoms continued, as well as others.

Unexplainably, I'd arrive at work feeling fine. Then later in the day, I would start to get a foggy feeling; leg cramps in the afternoon, as well as a feeling that I was choking. That pattern would continue until February 22, 2005, the last day I worked with Dennis.

One possible explanation I came up with after Dennis' arrest was that he might have gradually been poisoning me. In a later chapter, I will detail how he could have done this.

I was with some friends at a bar when this guy walked in. Even though he looked and sounded like Sam Waterston from the TV show *Law & Order*, I had this feeling that I wanted to get to know him really well, perhaps even to the point of marriage.

Well, I married Rod in December 2003, and the marriage was annulled in May 2004—the same month Dennis locked the door and came toward me with his eyes glazed like he was in a trance or something.

Rod annulled the marriage when his best friend convinced him that I was crazy. Part of it was Rod's fault; part my fault. I got this gut feeling while at work on this particular day, so after getting off work I drove through the parking lot of where Rod's ex-wife lived, and lo and behold, there was Rod's vehicle. I tried to talk to him about it, but once again I over-reacted—he said I was full of crap—and verbally unloaded on him.

I left and went to his mother's house—I had a key—and crawled into the guest bed. I had called my parents and they were on their way to get me, when Rod's friend called me, and said he just wanted to talk. He wanted me to tell him where I was. The next thing I knew the police showed up, and I was taken to the hospital for evaluation of a suicide attempt—there was no suicide attempt. The next day I was released. The doctor said, "You have no business being here."

When Rod realized his friend was acting out of jealousy of him spending so much time with me, he proposed again to me, and we were engaged when Dennis was arrested.

Twenty-eight: "It wasn't funny"

When I first started my job with the Compliance Department, I was given keys to the City of Wichita Animal
Shelter—that's where we took animals that we picked up.
The keys were because they closed at 6:00 p.m., and at
times we would get called out at odd hours for an animal
call, and might need to take one to the shelter.

There were also two incinerators there for dispensing
of the dead animals. When you pulled into the bay, to
the left, was another room separated by a door. Then
another door on the other side that housed these incinerators. I hated this room. It was creepy.

One time I was down there after hours as were two
other animal control officers from Sedgwick County. I
took a dead animal into the incinerator room, not knowing
that the door locked behind me. Well, I guess I don't
have to tell you that I freaked out and started banging on
the door. The other officers opened the door and were
laughing.

"It isn't funny," I said. I shook and had tears in my
eyes. They stopped their laughing for the moment.

When I told Dennis about the incident, he told me that
in the same room there was yet another door that led
outdoors.

After this happened, I suggested to my friend Penny
and the Court Clerk David that this would make a good
background for a Stephen King novel.

After Dennis was arrested, I thought just like all the
other animal control officers did:

*I wonder if Dennis disposed of evidence in the incin-
erators since they were usually running all the time.*

He had access 24 hours a day, seven days a week,
just as I did. I had keys to City Hall, the alarm clock, keys
to the shelter, and so did Dennis. Another thing that we
had were police radios—Dennis got to the point where he

took his home with him. Our radios were set up so that we could scan and listen to any channel—Wichita, Sedgwick County, Park City, Tac channels, EMS, the fire departments. If something was going on, we could listen to that beat in Wichita if we wanted to—just like the Police Department.

After his arrest, the *Wichita Eagle* asked Park City Police Chief Ball [he became Chief when my father retired] if Dennis had access to a police radio. Ball replied by saying that Dennis did not have access to police channels.

That statement was one of the bigger piles of bullshit dropped in Sedgwick County during those days!

My sister Michelle—during the years I worked with Dennis—worked with Paula at *Snacks* in Park City. Paula was a bookkeeper; Michelle a clerk. Paula had Michelle empty her wastebasket. Dennis would put all the paper that needed to be shredded in a laundry basket, and I would have to carry the laundry basket to another part of the building to shred paper.

Dennis had overtime every week. So did his wife, Paula. They went into work early, and left late. Although Dennis was a supervisor he was not salaried. I recall that on one two-week pay period he had 21 hours of overtime. I know this because he told me.

Even Paula had access to the police radio.

Michelle told me that Paula commented that she liked for Dennis to bring it home so that she could listen to the police traffic on the Park City channel. In my opinion, that gave Paula one-up on the gossip at work.

All this just goes to show you that no one watched Dennis.

For someone who was so consistent in putting in for overtime pay, Dennis was just as consistent in shirking his duty, especially if there was any chance he'd get his lotion-softened hands dirty.

Here is a classic example:

It was January 2004—about two months before BTK emerged with a series of *BTK Grams* and letter taunts to the police. We had a complaint regarding a man that smelled like cat urine—horribly so.

The thought of the complaining party was that he had a lot of cats.

Dennis assigned me to the complaint. I first went to the house where the man lived with his father. It was a two-story older home with a detached garage. I knocked on the door. No one was home. I then walked around the property and could count eight cats in the windows of the house.

You see, Park City had an ordinance regarding the limitations on animals—three dogs, three cats—anything over that was a violation.

I walked to the garage—the doors were open—and observed heat lamps set up inside. I also observed empty cat food cans and a lot of them—over a hundred of them—as well as makeshift bedding for animals.

I then went to the local grocery store and discount store and requested the information on the amount of cat food purchased in a week's time. I returned to the office and did my math, coming up with the possibility of at least 50 to 60 cats.

Next, I approached Dennis about the fact that if we have over 19 cats the State of Kansas could step in to assist us with the cost instead of the citizens of Park City eating the $16 per cat impound fee, plus the possible additional $15 per cat for putting them down.

The previous year I'd taken training, which a representative from the State of Kansas Animal Control gave, and I learned that they were there to assist us with the larger problems involving what they called *collectors*

Well, Dennis got indignant, probably because I knew something he didn't, but he told me to run it past Jack, which I did. Of course, Jack knew the importance of the burden this could place on Park City tax payers, so he told me to go ahead and make the call to the state, which I also did.

About a week later I was alerted that the state had done preliminary investigation enough to get a search warrant on the house. We were also told that the house was not in a habitable condition for humans.

The state was going to take care of the cat situation. However, the Park City Police Department would be called to assist on the serving of the warrant, and that the Compliance Department should be on standby for the Housing Code violations.

So here we are:

An attorney for the State of Kansas, State of Kansas Control officers, Park City Chief of Police and four or five Park City Police Department officers, and myself on standby outside of the house for the call from the State of Kansas Officers that there were housing code violations.

Meanwhile, Dennis is sitting in his office with his house slippers on in front of his PC either making his form of the day or working on his scrapbook, having made the statement, "If it's an emergency, call me."

So after the warrant was served, the standby officers began to enter the house—they got as far as opening the kitchen door when one of the officers yelled at me that there were some code violations as he was backing out of the house. At that time I was allowed to enter.

Picture this in your mind:

Three inches of cat poop on the stove, and on the floor in every room.

All of us thought we were going to have to burn our uniforms because of the stench.

After seeing the kitchen, I called Dennis. He calmly said, "What do you want me to do?"

So I called Jack and asked him to come see it for himself so that we could pull the occupancy permit. Jack quickly arrived and only made it as far as the kitchen. He called Judy back in the office to make the placards to be placed on the doors that stated:

THIS HOUSE IS NOT FIT FOR HUMAN OCCUPANCY

I took 57 photos that day, all the while gagging from the smell as everybody else was doing, while Dennis sat in the office. Representatives of four different law enforcement agencies and I did his job.

There were many instances like that one: that if it involved horrendous conditions, Dennis couldn't be bothered. In his mind, his job was more important than that of the Chief of Police.

"This guy was the prototype serial killer—he had a plan and stuck to the plan.

When it came to killing, he was very disciplined.

When it came to being a human, he was one of the worst examples ever.

He knew the difference between right and wrong, and he chose personal pleasure."

Dan Lickey
former Park City policeman

Twenty-nine: "Looked guilty as sin"

"I still kick myself in the butt for not picking up on the signs—that here was a guy acting like he had something to hide. Like everybody else, I just passed him off as being a weirdo—he's just being Dennis."

This comment was made by my friend Dan Lickey, who worked for the Park City Police Department when my father was Police Chief. He stayed with the Department awhile longer after Chief Ball took over. Dan has a unique perspective concerning Dennis Rader, whom he had to work with and put up with at times.

I will let Dan share his perspective with you.

Dennis is kind of a cold fish. Oddball. This guy is different but he never threw up a red flag that he was a criminal or that he was violent. He came across as sort of *nerdish*.

He'd say, "Hello, sir, how are ya?" But it was more robotic than sincere. He seemed ill at ease in social situations. He had this fake laugh . . . sort of like Jim Carey when he'd go, "Henh, henh, henh."

It was a creepy laugh, but at the same time, it was like Dennis was telling himself *Gee, I got to try and fit in here . . . let 'em know I'm a human being.*

He wanted to have control of a situation, even when the police were in control. And he was not able to see any fun in any situation. No, with him it was all over-serious. He just wasn't open to entertaining other aspects.

Here's an example of classic Dennis.

One time, I was at a home to help defuse a potential situation between Dennis and a woman he wanted to cite for letting her dog get loose. The lady said something like, "Believe me, I will have the dog secure and locked up tonight in the garage." But she said it more like a jest. She was totally cooperative.

Dennis started to read her the riot act. I interrupted him. "Dennis, she's joking."

"Oh," he said, "She's joking . . . henh, henh, henh."

He came across like he was not human . . . like an alien who suddenly learned what humor is and tried to show he knew what humor was by laughing. I'm sure that lady was creeped out by Dennis. I'm just glad I was there to keep the situation calm and under dignified control.

If you asked him anything, he would start to spiral up and ask, "So why are we doing it this way?" Like he was losing control of *his* operation. His eyebrows would furrow, and he'd get angry. Luckily, he didn't ask for our help very often.

Dennis couldn't get elected dogcatcher. He had to be appointed. I don't know how he was when he was off the job. I can only go by my personal experiences with him. He definitely believed his way was the only way. He was about as flexible as set concrete.

The following situation will show you what I mean.

Chief Ball called me on the radio. "Come up to the park...Dennis might need you to shoot an animal . . . and you're the best shot."

I get to the park. Dennis was there. The Chief was there.

Two teenage girls had been bitten by a kitten that had taken refuge up behind a rear tire in the transaxle area of an SUV. I don't know why, but each girl had reached up under there trying to get the kitten, which apparently wanted to be left alone. The skin was broken in each case, making it a concern whether or not the kitten had rabies. Bottom line: either we catch or kill the kitten, or both girls would have to take rabies shots.

Dennis had his control stick with a noose on the end so he could get it around the kitten's neck, and he had a net.

I had my shotgun and was ready, but by this time a big crowd had gathered; people and children were everywhere.

Dennis tried to get the kitten but it bolted and was off running.

To me, because of all the people, I figured I'd let the kitten run for a bit, and it would probably stop a few times and look around, and then I'd shoot it when there was no possible danger of any pellets hitting anyone. We were in a parking lot between the pool and the playground.

Dennis started screaming, "Shoot it! Get it! Kill it!"

His voice ratcheted up several octaves. He was excited, his words coming in staccato bursts. He scared children and adults. I'm thinking, *This cat just wants to get away from the hubbub.*

We're running, and he repeats, "Shoot it now! Kill it!"

I tell him, "Dennis, calm down. It will be okay."

He doesn't calm down. He shouts, "Well . . . give me the shotgun, and I'll—if you're not going to do it, then give me the shotgun, Goddammit!"

It was the first time I'd ever heard Dennis curse.

Firmly, I repeated, "Dennis, calm down!"

Dennis stopped and went back to his truck.

I followed the cat for another 50 or 60 yards. Then it decided to run up a tree where it'd be a static shot. It was clinging to the trunk, maybe ten, twelve feet up a huge old elm tree. It was a safe shot, so I took the shot, hitting the cat in the abdomen.

Dennis came running up. "Oh, you didn't shoot the head. Good."

He scooped the cat up and put it in a bag, and then said, "Oh, hey, sorry about that back there . . . henh, henh, henh."

And he was gone.

The two teenage girls did not have to take the rabies shots.

The one episode that sticks out the most in my mind happened in the spring of 2003, about ten or eleven months before Dennis wrote that letter to the *Eagle*, letting the world know that BTK was back.

I admit that I had bought into the notion that BTK must be fairly intelligent. I don't see how anyone could equate Dennis with high intelligence. Plus, he just didn't come across as a guy who could pull off the Otero murders by himself. The conventional wisdom was that, because dad and mom had martial arts training, that:

No. 1—it had to be more than one person;

No. 2—had to be someone who'd killed before; and,

No. 3—there was so much semen, that some detectives speculated that this was proof of possibly more than one person involved—OR the killer spent hours ejaculating over and over.

Anyway, on that spring day in 2003 Larceny had been committed—some ceramic art had been stolen out of somebody's front yard about a block from where Dennis lived. A culvert—what some people might call a glorified drainage ditch; actually, it is a tributary to Chisholm Creek—angled through the block, passing right behind the back of Dennis' property.

I thought I'd make a quick, but thorough inspection along the bank of this little creek, which splits the neighborhood like an alley. Well, Dennis could see me systematically checking behind his house, checking out his yard from the public side of the fence separating his property from the creek.

Dennis was on vacation that week. He comes out running with a trot, his eyes big, wide open. I'm thinking *Here he comes, sticking his nose in Police business.*

"Well . . ." he spluttered. "Wha—what are you doing?"

It was very out of character; not the usual robot saying, "Well, hello, sir . . . goodbye."

But because it was Dennis, I chose my words more professionally, just wanting him to go away and let me do my job. So I said, "I'm conducting an investigation."

He looked like he'd been hit in the stomach. His voice suddenly turned weak.

"Inves—investigation . . . into what?"

"Some kids stole something."

Air whooshed from him like the weight of the world had lifted from his shoulders. A smile creased his face. "Well, okay . . . henh, henh, henh . . . I thought I'd just see if I could come out and help."

He immediately turned around and went back into his house.

I sometimes think about this incident in retrospect: his roller-coaster emotions, and him looking guilty as sin. If I would have said, "I think you're BTK," I don't think I could have shocked him any more.

I would have to say that the worst times working under Dennis Rader's supervision were when I was not in a relationship. It wasn't until Jim Mies, my fiancé, told me in a joking manner that had I gone out with him back in the fall of 2002, Dennis probably would have never bothered me again. His comment set off a train of thought going back over the years, and I would have to say that he was correct.

You see, although Dennis bullied and harassed me, it was always worse when I wasn't in a relationship. It had gotten bad in 2001 when I was separated from Bob, my third husband. That is when all the medical problems started, such as my legs feeling paralyzed.

It was early March 2002 when I and Bob separated again, which ended up being permanent. The health problems again flared up.

I started seeing Rod in September 2002, and Dennis toned down his hatefulness. Rod and I had a rocky relationship so whenever we split, things were bad with Dennis.

My son Kyle lived with me at the time, and one day he asked me why Dennis was parked less than a block from our house—he was across the street less than a block away, and remained there for more than thirty minutes. I figured that he was spying on me since he was in his city vehicle—and there were no visible violations.

Bottom line was that Dennis always made my life hell at work when I wasn't in a relationship.

Jim is right. I realized this after recalling Dennis' own words that, after his fight with Kevin Bright, he never wanted another male in the picture.

Dennis steered clear of Jim and never dared mess with him. If there were ever any possible violations on Jim's business property, Dennis would have just let it be.

Jim wears the history of his younger years from body building and weightlifting on his arms.

Thirty: The nightmares begin

One time Dennis brought in a necklace that was made of black string and had a skunk on it. He also brought in white beads and black beads. He put the necklace on the bulletin board between his and my area, informing me that the white beads were for me, and the black ones for him.

You see, they had a busy season with skunks the summer before his arrest. When a skunk was spotted running loose during the day we were sent to resolve the problem. If I went out and verified that, indeed, there was a skunk then I'd contact the Park City Police Department—the PD—to assist me in putting the skunk down. Then I'd be responsible for disposing of it.

Well, according to Dennis, that entitled me to a white bead on the necklace.

Imagine the look on my face while a 59-year-old man was telling me this child's game he was going to play—and which he did play. He would add the beads to the necklace, and at times made comments like, "You're going to catch up with me."

On top of that, Dennis informed me that he'd made copies of the city map and wanted me to use a color highlighter to indicate what streets I drove while on patrol. What this entailed was when I returned from a patrol, I was to use a different color highlighter to color in the streets that I drove that day, and I was to coordinate the color with the time.

Was this some kind of device so that he could begin to stalk me? I have no way of knowing, but someone once pointed this possibility out to me.

I went to Jack, who of course talked to Dennis about the reason behind it. And, of course, Dennis being the slick SOB that he was, offered some stupid reason that convinced Jack to let him continue the practice.

So . . . here I was—a grown adult—playing connect the dots daily and wondering if I was in Hell. It was at such times that I marveled at Dennis' ability to even attain the job he had. It also made me further ask myself, *Am I crazy? Or is the entire city government crazy?*

This was barely a few weeks after the episode in May 2004 when Dennis had blocked my exit from the room

Looking back, I think another possibility was that all this bullshit was smoke and mirrors to keep me from having the time to figure out that Dennis was BTK. And I think he most certainly figured his games would keep Jack out of his hair—and he was right.

BTK had emerged from 13-plus years of silence via a letter to the *Wichita Eagle.* The letter was postmarked March 17, 2004. A lot of people thought he'd either died or simply disappeared somewhere into an incognito life. It jolted me back to remembering the atmosphere of fear that permeated Wichita, especially in the late 1970's.

But to one man—Gordon Wegerle—it was the vindication he'd hoped and prayed for so many years, ever since his wife Vickie had been murdered on September 16, 1986. No longer would people whisper behind his back, *I heard that he killed his wife...*

For Mr. Wegerle it was a day long overdue.

The truth was finally revealed.

The envelope that was turned over to the Wichita Police Department on March 19, 2004 bore the return address:

Bill Thomas Killman
1684 S. Oldmanor
Wichita, KS 67218

Initials: BTK

The serial killer was back, and this was just the first of a barrage of BTK Grams that Dennis Rader would send or leave in particular places for people to find.

This envelope contained photo copies of three Polaroid photographs of a bound female lying on a floor, and a Kansas Driver's License issued to Vicki Wegerle.

I felt a great sense of relief for Mr. Wegerle, but I was also ticked as hell that BTK was back. I felt I knew who BTK was—just could not put all of the pieces of the puzzle together, yet I knew that I somehow had the answer somewhere in my head. I just couldn't shake that answer out.

It was around the time of BTK's re-emergence and my boss' action in blocking my exit from our office, that the nightmares started. They frightened the crap out of me. My psychologist would tell me during our counseling sessions after Dennis' arrest that my subconscious was screaming, sensing danger.

The hair stands up on my neck, even now, just thinking about that first nightmare.

A couple that could be described as upper class, maybe in their late forties or early fifties, were standing inside the doorway to their home. They were reporting their 16-year-old daughter missing.

I was standing with the police officers taking the report. I'm listening to the father talk, as he wrapped his arm around his wife's shoulders, and she was sobbing great mournful sobs.

The officers were buying the story that the girl had run away. I was screaming, "They're lying! They're lying!" but the officers couldn't hear me or see me. I went into the house as they continued to talk to the couple.

As I walked around the house, I went to the master bathroom where there was a large stainless steel tub. The tub was stained in a purplish color that I knew was caused by blood.

I went running to the basement where I found a chest-deep freezer. When I opened it I found a lot of packages wrapped in white butcher's paper. I opened one of the packages. The couple had chopped up their daughter.

The next instant I was again standing near the doorway to the house, screaming, "They killed her! They chopped her up! Can't you see? They're lying! They're lying!"

But I couldn't get anybody to hear me or see me. The police officers believed the man and the woman and made a case for their daughter being a runaway.

I woke up; my heart racing, beating so hard I thought it would burst through my chest. I told my fiancé Rod, and later that day my Aunt Ruth and Sylvia at work, and my mother—but everyone just shook their heads and went back to whatever it was they were doing.

Dennis Rader admitted to detectives that the ultimate purpose of his flurry of BTK Grams—from March 2004 and continuing right on into February 2005—was to terrorize.

"I wanted to deliver the message that I had been all over, you know—I was omnipresent, and there was no place in Kansas that you were really safe if I was on the prowl."

Thirty-one: His huge ego

Like I said, I had stood my ground vs. Dennis until that last year. I don't know how to explain it, but it was like something inside of me put the brakes on my ability to stand that ground. Whatever it was, it compelled me to stay out of his sight as much as possible.

There were an increasing number of times that I felt lucky to get a full two weeks' paycheck, because I was calling in sick so much. He was getting more and more creepy. I hated to be around him.

That something inside of me was warning me—my hair would actually stand on end when he walked past my desk. It wasn't so much what he did as it was the vibe I was picking up. It was like I was sharing office space with Satan himself. I could feel the evil, almost like it was emanating from him. Invisible. You could almost see it. Or smell it.

Those last several months, Dennis put a lot of time into gardening, digging and planting big plants in the yard of his home at 6220 Independence. He lived in a little cookie cutter, ranch-style, wood frame, three-bedroom house that only had 960 square feet of livable space. I would later wonder what officials would find should they dig up that yard.

I just remembered something that happened later that year, in December 2004. A man was taken into custody as a person of interest in the on-going BTK investigation. Dennis was having the time of his life. He told me, "That man is going to have a hell of a lawsuit if they didn't arrest the right guy."

Looking back, that was a good day for Dennis. He was in a very good mood, and the only reason I think he was enjoying this was because he was getting worried that the authorities might be getting close to figuring out that he was BTK, and this threw them off the pass.

Meanwhile, BTK's insatiable thirst for publicity emboldened him to crank out a series of BTK Grams. Now that he'd gotten everybody's attention with evidence that he had murdered Vicki Wegerle, he was not about to fade away. He craved the limelight, and his huge ego spurred him on.

As the BTK Grams came on like corn popping, more and more people taxed their brains trying to figure out who the hell this guy was who seemed to gloat over his sick, cowardly exploits. There were even people meeting regularly in restaurant settings trying to do their best Sherlock Holms impersonations trying to solve the mystery. Many more people—not just in Kansas, but all over the map—were bloging on the Internet discussing possible clues.

I was in the presence of this evil, sensed the evil, felt the ever-increasing repulsiveness of being in the same office with Dennis—yet I was somehow blinded to the truth.

Did I want to find out what was in those files that Dennis never unlocked in my presence—and did I want to find out what was in that big Rubber Maid plastic container he'd been keeping under his desk of late?

You bet I did. But my growing fear of Dennis kept my curiosity in check. Any nerve left in my body was shot, frazzling more by the day.

Hindsight tells me that the most logical explanation for Dennis' trance-like visage when he blocked my exit from our office on that day in May 2004...was that he was mentally transforming back into BTK. I'm not positive, but that day might have been the same day—for sure, very close to the day—that Dennis mailed his second BTK Gram.

Thirty-two: MO-ID-RUSE

KAKE TV, Wichita's Channel 10, received a document in the mail on May 4, 2004, which was promptly turned over to the BTK serial killer task force. The envelope bore the return address of Thomas B. King, 408 Clayton St., Wichita, KS 67203. It was a simple rearrangement of the BTK initials of the previous BTK Gram delivered in March that year.

In the envelope were a word puzzle, photocopies of two identification cards, and a photocopy of a Special Officer badge, and a document titled *The BTK Story,* with a list of thirteen chapters.

The name of Francis Strong, supervising service foreman, Southwestern Bell Telephone Company, 622 East Central, was on one of the ID cards. Mr. Strong was interviewed and said he never possessed such an ID card, and that what detectives showed him was in fact a modified business card.

The Special Officer badge was made up to look like a Board of Education security badge. It had the name Larry Anderson on it. When interviewed, Galen Davis, director of security for the Board of Education, said the school district never used such a badge or issued such an identification card; further, that the only Lawrence Anderson that ever worked for the Board of Education died in April 1977.

As for Dennis' crude attempt at creating a mystifying puzzle that would consume hours of police time to solve, law enforcement quickly deciphered the puzzle, which was divided into three sections:

MO
ID
RUSE

Several words related to the subject were found in each section. Cruise, follow, prowl, and "go for it", for example, went in the MO section. In the ID section were entries such as officer, school, telephone co., Strong, and Anderson. The Ruse section included serviceman, handyman, insurance, realtor, and wrong address. Information on the identification cards correlated to the numbers in the puzzle.

I'm sure by this time that members of the BTK task force had to be discussing the possibility that whoever BTK was, he just might not be as smart as the original profiler's report speculated.

It amazed me that he could spell "ruse" but always seemed to pronounce it "russ."

Nine months later, task force detectives would learn what I already knew about Dennis L. Rader, which is that he is an idiot.

His own gullibility would do him in.

Especially while Dennis was plotting how and when to spring his next BTK Gram on authorities and a public that was once again feeling terrorized, he was still focusing on developing more codes to further clutter my routine.

I told you about his skunk and connect-the-dots-on-the-city-map games he played during the summer of 2004.

Do you realize how much I resent the fact that the City of Park City allowed him to play his BTK code game at work, and shove it down my throat?

I was forced to participate in this damn code game he had, only to find out later that he was BTK. It just sickens me. You know, I wonder if his family had codes at home. For example: GTS for "Gone to store." Or HAGD for "Have a good day." It wouldn't surprise me if that was the type of notes that Dennis left for his family.

Thirty-three:
Death on a Cold January Morning

Sometime early in the morning of June 13, 2004 Dennis duct-taped a clear plastic bag around the pole of the stop sign at the southeast corner of 1st and Kansas. Michael Hellman discovered the package on his way to work that morning. He removed an envelope from the plastic bag and took it with him. Once at work, he showed the envelope to his supervisors. He followed the instructions of Pamela Harmon to call the police.

On the front of the envelope were typed the words *BTK Field Gram*.

There was a document inside the envelope titled "C 1 Death on a Cold January Morning." There were four pages of the chapter on a reduced size piece of paper. Two pages of the chapter were on another piece of paper. There was a drawn picture of a nude, bound and gagged woman hanging from a rope. A photo caption said, "The Sexual Thrill is My Bill." In the bottom right hand corner of that piece of paper was the identifying BTK symbol. There also was a list of chapters of the BTK Story as mentioned in the MO-ID-RUSE envelope sent by BTK the previous month.

In horrific detail, BTK described the cowardly murders of the Oteros. Dennis apparently had attempted to write the story of his exploits in novel format on February 3, 1974, the month after he murdered four members of the Otero family. I will only include in this chapter some details that were not told in Dennis' own words back in chapter four: "Evil descends".

Dennis called himself *Rex* in his pitiful excuse of a novel. Here are some excepts as written by Dennis, including his bad spelling, grammar and punctuation.

[The} fantasy of having a pretty bound victim before his hand . . . [T]he natural sex appeal of girl and fantasies of them bound and torture, or mainly just being helpless grew each day inside his body. Soon, just the thought of a girl being bound was enough. He could play with himself and think and immediately have an ejection [sic] .
. . . Eventually the long years of fantasy, the thinking and desire boil over and in one night he began to stake his prey.

[He detailed the planning and preparation for the Otero murders.]

Now next to garage, he has to think, there was only one way you kept ahead of the police, and that was to think hard . . . . He decided to take the woman inside the house with the two kids. . . . He first, quietly try the back door but it was lock, so he settled down near the door. Removing wire cutter he gently snip the telephone cord, placed a nylon mask on, withdrew a knife, checked his gun and waited.

Finally, about twenty minutes before nine the door opened, and the boy step outside, in just a flash he order him back inside, confronting the family armed with a pistol and knife he told them that this was a stick up and not to be alarmed.

The family was preparing to leave, the kids were packing their lunchs [sic] and had gather [sic] their coats by the table. . . . The boy was by his folks side looking scared and the girl, Josephine was beginning to cry.

[The family dog interrupted.]

Rex wanted the pest out and told them he would shoot it or them if they try any funny tricks. Expressing that the gun he held was an automatic and hollow points bullet that would kill Joe, reasure his that if the dog was out of the way, things would be better. So, agreeing the man let Joe [the young son] put the dog out, but being very careful of Joe [the father].

[The *author* went on in great detail, obviously relishing the reliving of the murders, how he murdered the mother, father, and son, before taking little Josephine down to the cellar where he hanged her. He concluded this portion of his "novel" as follows.]

[Josephine] stared at him and brink [sic] hard as he reach down and slip the noose around her neck, and quickly pulled her up right, she turn in the rope gasps and bink hard as the rope tighten and she died. . . He pulled her sweat shirt up and with sexual relaxation masturbated on her and in his handkerchief . . . the dream had come true.

Come to think of it, Dennis did give me a gift once besides the snowman ornament pictured on the back cover of this book. But it was not at Christmas time.

It was a bumper sticker:

So many cats. So few recipes.

I thought the bumper sticker was merely another example of Dennis "just being Dennis." However, looking back, the gift of the snowman ornament scared the hell out of me. I think that in his mind he thought he was smarter than me, and this was a way to play mind games with me.

As he picked out this ornament I believe he was envisioning choking me with a long woolen, winter scarf. I think his plans to hang and stretch victim No. Eleven from the ceiling were already cemented in his mind.

Absolutely, I believe that this No. Eleven—Project Broadwater—was to be me, and I've told you why. And I think that he planned to gag and bind me before asking me, "Remember that snowman ornament with the scarf around its neck?"

Thirty-four: Three more in 2004

Dennis prepared and left three more packages that year:

A two-page story entitled "Jakey" was found in a plastic bag at the bottom of the library book return box on Saturday morning, July 17. "BTK FLASH GRAM" was on the title page of five sheets of paper.

The story of *Jakey* was about the death of Jake Allen in Argonia, Kansas. The package contained photocopies of four pictures of a male in bondage. Work on the BTK Story, the author said, had to stop because of Allen's death:

"I was so excited about this incident that I had to tell the story."

The author claimed involvement in the young man's death by hanging.

"Jakey had fantasies about Sexual Masturbation in unusual ways with Bondage and Homosexual thrills. . . . When I peck [type] this out my Sparky is going hard ....Now back to Chapter Two. May not made the July deadline, be patient."

Earlier in the epistle, the author confessed, "I'm much older (not feebler) now and have to conditions myself carefully. Also my thinking process is not as sharp as it uses [sic] to be."

He warned, "I have spotted a female that I think lives alone. . . I think fall or winter would be just right for the HIT."

The next plastic bag was found near the UPS drop box outside of the Omni Center office building at 200 North Kansas in the evening of October 22. The plastic bag contained an envelope titled *BTK FIELD GRAMS*.

Again, as always with bona fide packages from the serial killer, there was BTK's personal identifying mark. Picture a horizontal, upside down capital B with a dot in the middle of each enclosure to make it look like a woman's breasts. The top line of this upside down B is the top line of a capital T. A capital K is also horizontal and looks like it is holding up the "breasts" of the capital B. The T extends down through the middle of the K.

In this package was the document purporting to tell the story of BTK. Authorities filed this package as C2.DAWN, probably because the author's list of chapters included "Chapter 2: Dawn."

There also was a montage of photocopies of pictures of children, apparently cut from magazines. Over the pictures were hand-drawn bondage depictions including gags.

Then on December 8, 2004 a man called Brandon Sauer, manager of the Quik Trip at 3216 East Harry. The unidentified man told Sauer, "I'm calling to tell you of a BTK package at Ninth and Minnesota on the Northeast corner." Mr. Sauer was directed to write down a set of instructions and read them back. The store manager called police, who were unable to find the package.

Five days later, while walking through Murdock Park, William Ronald Ervin found a white trash bag containing a clear plastic bag. Inside the bag were a doll, papers, and an ID for Nancy Fox. Mr. Ervin's mother recognized the name as a BTK victim. The Ervins called KAKE TV and a cameraman filmed the package, which was turned over to the police.

On an index card attached to the package was written *Dollgram*

"CHAPTER 9: HITS: PJ FOX TAIL – 12-8-1977" described in minute detail the murder of Fox. The small doll in the package was trussed up to resemble how BTK had bound Fox.

During his interrogation on February 25 and 26, 2005, Dennis admitted to being a poor student in college.

"I was probably about a D plus or a C minus type person when I was in college . . . but my grades weren't that good. I'm not a good speller. You probably already know that. In fact, my wife (Paula) said to me the other day, she said, 'You spell just like BTK.'"

Thirty-five:
Strange doings before the fall

January 2004 arrived and with it the REALLY weird Dennis.

People are creatures of habit—so after six-and-a-half years working with Dennis, I could set my watch to his activities. I could tell you the time without looking at the clock just based off his routine. I guess there was some feeling of security—although very little—in knowing in advance just about everything Dennis would do on any given day—at least when and how he did things.

That all suddenly changed with the New Year. The new, unpredictable Dennis had replaced the predictable Dennis. Until then, if something did come up, at least Dennis would call or have his wife Paula call to get a message to Jack or me.

On the first occasion when Dennis was late, I went up front and asked Beth, the receptionist, if Dennis had called; and then I asked the rest of the girls in the office— no one had heard from him.

I returned to my desk and in walked Dennis as if everything was normal and he wasn't late. I felt a chill of evil as he walked past my desk.

On another occasion in February he was about two hours late. My gut knotted up, and I vividly recall my feeling of dread when Dennis came in—once again there were no calls, and I had the same eerie feeling.

He did other things that were not in character with his previous predictable habits. He started walking around the City Hall building during his afternoon 15-minute break, and he was always swinging his arms in front of him and over his head.

Later it would dawn on me that BTK was getting in shape to kill again.

There were times—especially during that last month—that Dennis would disappear in the building. In the past, I would never have given it a second thought, but now, for some reason, I felt compelled to see if I could find him. I'd later thank God that I never could.

After it was all over and everything had come out into the open as to BTK's identity, I wondered, *What was he doing?*

I determined that he was down in the basement listening to conversations through the vents. After the new section of the building was built, there were some flaws where full conversations could be heard both directions through the vents. Dennis must have been really paranoid to find out if anyone was talking about him, and if they suspected him.

I'd had previous conversations with Dennis about BTK. In 2004, right after BTK had popped up again, he'd even showed me a police artist rendering based on a description Kevin Bright gave police back in the 1970's. He brought the drawing over to my desk and said, "That looks like me...I could be BTK." He smirked and went back to his desk.

I just chalked it up to Dennis being weird.

It was after he was arrested, and they put his picture and the sketch next to each other on TV that, indeed, you could see that it was the same beady eyes—it was Dennis Rader.

In early February 2005 I had turned in my resignation as an employee for the City of Park City, Kansas.

Dad and Jack talked me out of it—Dad reminding me of how bad the job market was at that time in Wichita and surrounding areas, and asking me how in the hell could I support myself and my son Kyle without a job, and without medical coverage? Jack said—again—that he would do something about Dennis.

I was caught between that famous rock and a hard place. I caved in, telling myself, *Maybe Dennis will retire and life at City Hall won't be so bad.*

When Dennis found out about me not going ahead and quitting, he was angry. I'm sure he had prepared himself mentally to make a second attempt at killing me. He'd been thwarted the first time when city crews were working on the curbs in my neighborhood, and had retreated, waiting for another day to carry out the hit. It would make things easier for him were I no longer an employee at City Hall. I even think he figured that my on-again-off-again relationship with Rod might make Rod a suspect. I know this sounds bizarre, but that's how Dennis' excuse of a mind worked.

On that same day, out of the blue, I still don't know why, but I asked him a question about Marine Hedge, who had been murdered on April 27, 1985 and lived only a few houses down the street from his house. That murder had not yet been connected to BTK.

I spoke out very audibly, "Hey, Dennis..."

"Yes," he replied, focusing those dead beady eyes on me.

"How did Paula respond when Marine Hedge was murdered?" I said.

He seemed startled by the question. He got up from his chair and walked slowly toward my desk as he replied. "It scared the daylights out of her. . . . Why do you ask?"

"No reason . . . just curious," I said.

Although he didn't say any more and returned to his desk, I'm sure I unknowingly added to his feelings of paranoia. I'm also sure that this further fueled his desire to get rid of me. I think he was starting to get jumpy over seeing his own shadow.

More and more I had the feeling that Dennis was there in the office, but somehow he wasn't there. He seemed increasingly lost in thought. I later realized that this probably had a lot to do with his communications with the media and the Wichita Police Department during January and February.

Remember when I told you that BTK always seemed to be active around my birthday?

Well, it was on February 2, 2005—my 45th birthday—that I typed up my resignation stating that February 18th would be my last day.

I was pissed because not only was it horrible but I was the only Park City employee who didn't even receive the minimum 2.5 percent increase.

Zip.

I put a copy of my resignation letter in Dennis' in-box, one in Jack's and gave one to Carol Jones for my file.

Later that afternoon Dennis called me into his office. He was sitting in front of his computer and in an unusually good mood. He said he was typing an acceptance letter to my resignation. He wanted to be sure that I understood that between then and the 18th what I would be allowed to do—he wanted me to do only animal control.

Jack called me into his office later that afternoon and asked me to reconsider—that he understood I was mad about my review and working for Dennis. He said I should once more try to do a grievance.

I replied that Dennis was already typing the acceptance letter to my resignation.

"Dennis does not have the authority to do that," Jack said.

I thought it over and the next day I typed a letter rescinding my resignation, and decided to start with another grievance.

Dennis was angry at me for reconsidering.

He was angry at Jack for talking me out of leaving.

Before Dennis was arrested, I had a conversation with my brother, Hobert, who is a policeman in Park City. I told him about the incidents that were occurring at the duplex where I lived—the one located just off Broadway and behind which was located the lagoon.

His reply was, "Mary, that's your internal instinct kicking in—your sub-conscious telling you that something's wrong. It's what protects you because your conscious mind doesn't see it or want to see it. It's what keeps you alive and protects you."

Dennis overheard that conversation.

Thirty-six: His stupidity surfaces

I will reveal to you in the next chapter all the weird things happening where I lived; but first, I'll tell you what was going on between Dennis and the Wichita police. The sequence of events must have really frustrated Dennis, especially since one of his packages took so long to wind up in the hands of the police.

Dennis sent a postcard addressed to KAKE-TV 10 that was received on January 25. The return address was 803 N. Edgemoor, Wichita, KS 67208. That was the Otero family address.

On the back of the postcard, the writer stated a Post Toasties cereal box was located between "69th N and 77th N on Seneca St." Then the writer wrote, "Let me know some how if you or Wichita PD received this [and whether] you or PD received #7 at Home Depot Drop Site 1-8-05."

A TV film crew dispatched to the area described on the postcard found the cereal box on the side of the road. Detectives took possession of the cereal box. It contained a doll representing 11-year-old Josephine Otero. A rope wrapped around the doll's neck was tied to a curved piece of PVC pipe

Also among the cereal box contents were a two-page document titled "CHAPTER 9 HITS: PJ-LITTLE MEX-01-15-1974, BTK's acronym list, more chapters of the BTK Story, and two pages describing BTK's Haunts. There was also some jewelry inside the cereal box.

Once again, BTK gave details of the Otero murder scene. He was excited because "This was going to be BTK's 1st big Hit if things work out . . . An Organized Sexual Kiiler [sic] did the Murders; it is the true Sadistic Killer profile that happens here."

Detective Tim Relph contacted Bill Polzin, manager of the eastside Home Depot, who was very cooperative, offering all the assistance he possibly could in locating the missing package left there on January 8. Employees searched everywhere, but no such package was found.

And here's where the trail gets interesting.

Employee Edgar Bishop saw the notice posted in the employee break-room asking if an unusual package had been found by any employee. Bishop said that his roommate, Kelly Paul, had found a cereal box with writing on it in the bed of Bishop's pick-up truck about two weeks before.

The box was described as a Special K cereal box containing several pieces of computer paper and a blue beaded necklace. Bishop said he thought someone was playing a joke on him and he threw the box away. He said the trash had been hauled off to the dump.

But on January 27—two days later—Bishop reported that the cereal box was still in the trash because he had not put the trash out before going on vacation. Detectives recovered the box, which contained a document titled "BOOM," more info about the BTK Story, and a stunning document called "COMMUNCIATION."

The Home Depot security tape from January 8 showed a dark-colored SUV type vehicle, possibly a Jeep Cherokee, pulling alongside Bishop's truck. An unidentifiable person got out of the car and walked around Bishop's truck.

In the "BOOM" document, BTK described BTK's Lair—a three-story house with an elevator, and containing a kill room which the writer called "BTK's DTPG & BONDAGE ROOM." DTPG stood for "death to pretty girl." Also there was a list of BTK's projects, with focus again on Josephine Otero and Nancy Fox.

The document titled "COMMUNICATION" probably caused members of the BTK strike force to salivate. Whoever this guy was, he seemed to have unwittingly—

more like dumbly—provided a possible means to identify him.

WHAT AN IDIOT!!!!!

Dennis asked this question:

"Can I communicate with Floppy and not be traced to a computer? . . . Be honest."

He then told the police to run an ad "Under Miscellaneous Section, 494" in the newspaper; that the message should say, "Rex, it will be OK" if a "Floppy" cannot be traced.

Dennis promised a "floppy for a test run" soon.

Of course the Wichita Police Department ran the ad.

Dennis sent a postcard that was received February 3, 2005 by KAKE TV. He expressed thanks "for your quick response on # 7 and 8" and "to the News Teams for their efforts." He also informed "WPD that I receive the News-paper Tip for a go . . . Test run soon."

I can imagine what the detectives were thinking. The toned-down version might have gone something like this:

Three decades and we can't figure out who the SOB is, and now he's about to give himself to us on a silver platter.

The next—and the last—BTK-mailed envelope was received February 16 by Marcine Andrews, a receptionist for KSAS TV, Channel 24. It was a padded envelope with excess postage. I guess Dennis wanted to make damned sure the letter got through.

The return address was P.J. Fox, 316 N. West St., Wichita, KS 67203.

In the envelope were three index cards, a gold chain with locket, and a purple computer disk. One of the index cards contained an explanation about the diskette and instructions for further communication by means of another newspaper ad.

A forensic examination of the disk was performed by Detective Robert Stone. He found one valid file: "Test

A.RTF." It contained the words "This is a test. See 3 X 5 Card for details on Communication with me in the newspaper."

The properties section of the document revealed the name of Dennis and Christ Lutheran Church. Apparently within minutes, and following a Google search on the Internet for Christ Lutheran Church, detectives knew the following:

Dennis Rader was president of the congregation, and was a compliance officer for the City of Park City, and that he lived at 6220 North Independence in Park City. Detectives quickly drove by that address and observed a black Jeep Grand Cherokee parked in the driveway. The vehicle was registered to Brian Rader, the son of Dennis Rader.

Next a biological sample from a medical procedure on Kerri Rader, Dennis Rader's daughter, was obtained by Court order. Within days and after very extensive DNA testing of evidence collected during the original investigations of the murders that BTK had boasted of committing, authorities knew Dennis Rader was their man.

There was one brief moment of levity during the two-day sentencing hearing. It happened during Captain Sam Houston's testimony about the murder of Dolores Davis.

The prosecution's power-point presentation displayed a comment made by Rader during questioning after his arrest:

"I really wanted to spend some time with her; but damn it, she said, 'there's somebody coming.' I could not believe my luck in these places. I always got somebody coming."

I'm not sure of the exact verbal exchange between the prosecutor and Captain Houston, but as I recall, it went something like this:

"Captain Houston...Mr. Rader believed his victims when they told him somebody was going to show up?"

"He believed them like he believed us."

There was laughter in the courtroom. Everyone knew Captain Houston was referring to the floppy disk that police had told him could not be traced.

Thirty-seven: Timeline of terror

Here is a timeline of events from January 21, 2005 up until Dennis' arrest five weeks later on February 25.

January 21

Dennis walked over to my desk. He said that Jack had just told him that my annual review was due that day. Dennis was put out by this, and wanted a lot more time to review everything before completing my review. He said, "The city is never prepared...If I have to do it by the end of the day you are not going to be happy with it."

My review was rescheduled to January 24th.

January 24

Dennis gave me my annual review. It was less than satisfactory. I believed I was the only City Hall employee to not receive a raise. During the review, Dennis made several derogatory comments. At one point, anger rose in his voice; he glared at me and said, "I can't trust you."

January 25

I began finding the front porch light at my duplex apartment unscrewed almost daily.

February 3

Jack talked me out of my resignation. I changed my mind, pending a grievance against Dennis. When I got home from work, I noticed that the mini blinds in my living room were pulled away from the window and caught on some family pictures of my sons.

I lived alone. My skin started to crawl every time I got home from work. I thought *Who is doing this? If you are trying to freak me out, it's working.*

February 5
I received a Caller ID withheld call. The caller left a message. It was a man belching. (It was one of the first things that I recalled after Dennis' arrest. He belched all the time.)

February 7
When I returned home from work I found a puddle of water in the middle of my bathroom. There had been no water, no leak, zip, when I'd left that morning for work.

February 12
Received a Caller ID withheld call. The caller left a message. It was a man disguising his voice. The voice said that I was hot, and wanted kinky sex, and that the caller wasn't bi—just bi polar.

February 15
I stayed that night at Rod's house. I awoke from a deep sleep in the middle of the night, my heart racing, and gasping for breath. Rod woke up and asked me what was wrong. I told him that I felt like I was in great danger. I could not shake the feeling. It felt like every hair on my body was standing on end.

February 17
All that week I had this overwhelming creepy feeling that I was being watched, and that someone was trying to hurt me. I heard my brother, Hobert, on the police radio. I called him and asked that when he wasn't busy to come by the office. I told him of all the weird things, and how I couldn't shake this feeling of dread. That is the conversation that Dennis overheard.

February 21 and 22

Dennis and I worked together on those two days. They were the last two days that I worked with Dennis. February 21 was the day I'd asked him how his wife, Paula, had reacted after the Marine Hedge murder.

I could not shake the feeling of evil I felt as he slowly walked toward my desk, his eyes boring right through me.

February 23

I worked that day. It was the last day I actually worked on the job. Dennis was off that morning to take his mother to the doctor. He had always returned to work before after things like that. He did not return to work that day. That really spooked me out—so much so that I requested February 24 off as a floating holiday.

February 25

Dennis was arrested. I described in chapter one what I went through that day.

The face that wasn't there

My family is very close. Sometimes two or more of us have similar feelings at the same time—call it a premonition, if you will. Mom and I both had experiences in the days before Dennis' arrest that some folks might call just plain spooky.

She heard some kind of noise in the back yard she'd never heard before. After checking the storage room, and finding nothing that could have made the sounds, she got chills. A feeling came over her that her son, Jeffery—the one that had committed suicide—was somehow trying to warn her about some danger to her family.

That was around the time that I woke up in the middle of the night sensing I was in grave danger. I believe that it was my brother that woke me up to get my attention that something was wrong.

Perhaps it was a guardian angel. All I know is that mom and I had similar feelings very close to the same day. So did my youngest sister Kim.

My sister Michelle experienced such feelings almost daily during the two weeks prior to Dennis' arrest. As she would open her front door, through the security screen she would see a face—how do you explain this other than the way I'm explaining it?—but the face wasn't there, not as a real face, but a very indistinct impression of a face that she could not see clearly or identify; it was never clear enough to tell who it was.

On the day Dennis was taken into custody, Michelle opened the door.

It was the face of Dennis Rader.

And that was one day before it was announced that my boss was the BTK killer.

Thirty-eight: Upsetting dreams

The dream I had the night I was awakened in the middle of the night at Rod's place gave me the feeling of raw terror; that I could not go anywhere to escape whatever it was that was coming after me to kill me.

Nightmares really set in about a week after Dennis' arrest. I hadn't slept that whole week. I kept reliving all the times that I'd said or done things that could have set Dennis off, and those times when Dennis said things that scared the hell out of me.

About two months before his outing as BTK, Dennis had walked over to my desk while I was working on my computer. He said, "Are you doing drugs or drinking?" A smirk from Hell was plastered on his face.

I looked up at him and said, "What the hell?"

Dennis didn't respond. He chuckled as he walked away.

It was on the second or third night of trying to sleep that the realization hit me:

All the symptoms I'd been plagued with had disappeared the week Dennis was arrested. No longer did I have that foggy feeling; leg cramps in the afternoon, and that feeling of choking. I'd gone through a number of months experiencing those symptoms, and they were progressively getting worse, especially those final few months. There'd been times when I was on patrol that my mind was so foggy I couldn't put two thoughts together. Other times it was like I'd just snapped out of a trance, wondering where I was. There even were times that I'd be driving and forget where I was going.

I suddenly had problems with my blood sugar drop-ping very low. Those symptoms also disappeared after February 23rd, my last day in the office. And no more weird things happened in my duplex apartment. This had to be more than just a coincidence.

My mood with my loved ones had become no longer amiable; instead, I'd become irritable, snapping at people, as well as being paranoid about everything.

I wondered, *Why did this happen? How did it happen?*

But now my mind was crystal clear, and I thought color coded, foil-wrapped chocolates. Everybody in the building knew that I liked chocolates. Dennis had surprised me by giving me some chocolates wrapped in foil. Looking back, I knew that was completely out of character for him to do that.

Then I thought drops in my ever-present can of Diet Pepsi that was always sitting on my desk.

BAM! I smacked myself in the head. I did some research that scared the daylights out of me.

TRANQ!

It must have been the *Tranq*, I reasoned. *Tranq* was short for the tranquilizer we used to bring down and control animals, but I could think of us only having to do that maybe one or two times a year—never more than several times a year. I found out that Dennis had made a lot of purchases of the *Tranq*.

Why so much?

I never came out and said that Dennis used the tranquilizer on me; all I wanted to do was see the files to see if there was any *Tranq* missing. Not getting the cooperation I sought, I conducted my own independent research. I found out that one of the drugs in the *Tranq* was Ketomine, which is used illegally as a date rape drug due to the immobilization affect it has—it affects the muscles and it causes amnesia.

It would have been easy for Dennis to use a small needle to push a small amount of *Tranq* into a chocolate, just enough to cause the symptoms I was going through. It would have been even easier to doctor my Diet Pepsi.

I concluded that *Tranq* was a logical explanation for my symptoms and my drastic change in behavior.

I will follow up on this discussion in the next chapter.

It got to where I not only had trouble getting to sleep; I dreaded going to sleep because of the nightmares.

This is by far the dream that upset me the most. I swear it was as if Dennis was really there having a real conversation with me. It is a feeling I never want to have again.

I am pulling into my driveway. I get out of my car and walk up to my front door. But before I get to the front door . . . there is a window to the right, and I see fingers, from the knuckles down, holding open a section of the mini blinds. I look closer and I see Dennis' eyes and face.

I turn and run to my car and call 911 [Park City emergency].

"Help me, please!" I beg. "I need help!"

When the police get there they arrest Dennis as BTK. But he gets out on bail, and is allowed by the police department to come back to my house by himself to get his things that he had left behind.

He is wearing black trousers and a white, sleeveless undershirt—a wifebeater. As he is gathering his things, I ask him why he was so horrible to me at work, and why did he do the things that he did to those people.

During this conversation he is putting on a black suit jacket, and then puts on a hat that a chauffeur would wear. He opens a door leading underground, and gets on his hands and knees, and backs down the stairs and grabs his black murder bag, and he says,

"Because that is who I am. I am Evil."

The door slams shut, and he is gone.

The thing I find really spooky is that in this dream where Dennis is in my home, and he grabs his bag for murder—it was months later before it was disclosed to the public that Dennis had a bag he called his Hit Kit.

Two nights later I dreamed that everyone knew who Dennis was, yet he still had the job with Park City, and the city got him a new car which is a sports car that is yellow with red flames, and no one would listen to my complaints.

I went several nights before the next dream.

Dennis radios me to show up at a parking lot to assist him with capturing a dog. When I arrive, he tells me to go with him behind the building, that the dog had gone there; yet I know he is lying, and that he is trying to trap me behind there, so that he can kill me to keep me quiet.

One or two nights later I had another nightmare.

Dennis calls me to come by his house; that his wife, Paula, is going to take us to a location for a Pet ID Clinic that we were doing. When I arrive, Dennis is wearing the white undershirt again, instead of his uniform.

The inside of the house is a mess, and there are red drapes on the windows. Dennis is acting strangely; yet the three of us get into Paula's vehicle, with Paula driving. Dennis is sitting in the back seat; and I get in and sit in the front passenger seat.

As we are going down the road Paula whispers to me that Dennis is BTK, and that she is fed up. Dennis overhears her, and becomes angry.

I woke up and never knew the outcome of that dream. I did not want to know.

Some nightmares repeated, and I had other nightmares that merged together, creating endless situations that I couldn't possibly escape from. Many times I'd awake with a start, and look around to make sure that I was not still in the dream.

The nightmares grew in intensity again right after the sentencing hearing. I was having them even a year after my boss was exposed as the BTK serial killer. One that I vividly recall was in March 2006.

I hope you understand, but I have to get out of this chapter soon; so I will just tell you that it involved Dennis getting out of prison and coming after me.

My life today is one of pleasant dreams; not one of nightmares.

My life is a 180-degree turn from what it was during 2005. You know what I was doing the night before I wrote this?

I was taking the first night of lessons toward qualifying to take the test for my Kansas motorcycle driver's license. One of my fiancé's Harleys has my name on it.

You heard right.

My family has always called me Mary Nova. And I'm telling you—Mary Nova is back.

No more hiding from the public. I'm enjoying life again. I smile. I laugh. And, yes, I speak my mind. I'm helping my fiancé run his trucking company, which is many times the responsibility I had while working for Park City.

Did I mention that Mary Nova is back?

Thirty-Nine: "The door blew open"

When Dennis was arrested, I was told that all the files that the Compliance Department had stored down in the basement of City Hall, including all of the files for compliance in mine and Dennis' office, were placed in the area considered to be Dennis' office.

The room was then sealed per order of the district attorney. An official memo was placed on the interior door of that area stating as much.

Jack Whitson told me that the entire back area had been re-keyed, including the door that opened out behind City Hall—Dennis' private office entrance and exit.

Keep this in mind.

In March 2005, not long after Dennis was revealed to be BTK, Tad Wagner, my attorney, requested documents from the City, and he received a FAX from the City Attorney stating that they did not have them.

Mainly, Tad and I wanted to see the purchase records showing how much and how many times Dennis had put in orders for the *Tranq*. This would have at least given us an indication whether or not he might have been using the *Tranq* to cause the symptoms that I was having—the same symptoms that disappeared the week of his arrest.

My doctor and I would sure like an explanation for my sudden cure. I don't think it was a miracle.

Could it have simply been that Dennis was no longer able to slip *Tranq* into my Diet Pepsi, which, as I said, would have been quite easy to do?

And is that why I no longer felt so foggy mentally in the afternoons?

Tad made a simple, direct, logical request in my behalf. So why did the city attorney say they did not have the records? After all, Jack had told me that *all of the files* had been placed—and sealed—in the area considered to be Dennis Rader's office.

Again, my question is, If that is so, then what happened to the files? Where are they? Did someone take them, and, if so, when and how?

I wracked my brain, trying to figure out all the possibilities, logical and otherwise.

Tad and I later found out there had been a *non-forced break-in* into Dennis' office. A *non-forced break-in* meant that someone would have had to have the key to enter. It was reported that the exterior door to Dennis' office was open. This door was at the rear of the building and was not visible from the street.

Remember—Dennis had his own private entrance.

After word got out that people were aware of the initial report, and the media started asking questions, the police report was changed to state that the wind blew the door open.

Give me a break. We're talking about a steel door that's dead bolted.

My attorney shared this information with Carol McKinley, Fox News reporter, Denver correspondent. She was in town interviewing me. Her conversation with Tad was off the record. Anyway, a week later Tad and I were talking on the phone when he told me that McKinley had called him, and told him that she had to leave town, but that in regard to the information he had given her, she had asked a KAKE news reporter to go over and look at this door. The reporter did so, and found the story of the wind blowing it open to be unbelievable. Not only that, but the reporter found that the evidence tape was still intact.

Odd, isn't it?

My attorney and I managed to get copies of the front page of the police reports. We found out that Park City had requested that the Sedgwick County Sheriff's

Department do the report on the date of the alleged break-in.

And then later Park City changed its report, saying that the wind had blown the door open. Meanwhile, the Sheriff's Department did not change its report—it remained the same, citing a *non-forced break-in.*

I still mull over the possible implications of what all of this means. It seems to me to be a huge, huge stretch to believe that the wind blew open a locked, dead-bolted, steel door—a door that opens outward, not inward—that still had the evidence tape intact, according to the reporter that had examined the door. Now, keep in mind that I'm thinking out loud, so to speak. Let's consider that it is possible, as the reporter suspected, that the wind did not blow the door open.

What options does that leave?

I've thought it through and through, sometimes even waking up in the middle of the night; and the one conclusion that seems the most plausible is that someone could have gone into Dennis' office area from inside the building.

If I were a betting person, this last possibility is where I'd place my money.

Whatever really happened, and whoever went into Dennis' office area—did that person or persons remove the files before or after the city attorney told Tad that the city did not have the files?

Again, I am just thinking out loud.

Let me put it this way. If you had the same symptoms that I experienced—that were really evident during the afternoons—and you found out that your boss was a serial killer, and that after his arrest you never had those symptoms again—what would you do?

Oh, I forgot—and you knew he did the ordering and had ready access to the *Tranq* . . . and you did research that showed the *Tranq* contained a drug often used illegally in date rape drugs that could account for your symptoms—are you getting my drift?

I think you would want to know how much *Tranq* was in inventory, and how much your boss had been ordering.

What do I think?

I think that somebody knows how much *Tranq* Dennis Rader ordered—and also how much *Tranq* was on hand and how much was missing.

And, yes, absolutely, I think there was some kind of conspiracy to keep me, the media, and the public from finding out any clues that might indicate an employee of the City of Park City, Kansas might have misused a drug concoction meant to temporarily disable an otherwise uncontrollable animal.

Whew! That was a mouthful, but I had to spit it out.

But a nagging question remains:

Why all the secrecy and changing of reports if there was no break-in?

Maybe I will never penetrate what I believe is a well covered-up conspiracy. But I keep asking myself, *What could be so damaging that City Hall wanted to put a lid on it? What could be worse than the public already knowing that Park City had hired a serial killer and repeatedly gave him good job reviews?*

I do a lot of head shaking whenever my mind revisits this discussion.

I've often thought what a neat world this would be if everyone lived their life by the Golden Rule—treat others as you would have them treat you.

If everyone did, I never would have felt the need to write this book. Go back and read chapter one again, and tell me if Jack and the mayor treated me like they wanted me to treat them.

Forty: The aftermath

Post Traumatic Stress Syndrome
I'd always thought that was the tag reserved for military personnel stressed out after their harrowing experiences in Vietnam and Iraq.
Then the tag was put on me.
I'd already been terribly stressed out months before my boss was revealed to be BTK. But when Dennis was outted, an emotional dam broke, plunging me into deep depression.
However, I never reached the point where I just wanted to pack it in and give up on life. I'm just too darned stubborn to do that.
I'm a fighter . . . a survivor.

After Dennis was arrested, and I started seeing a doctor to talk about everything, he gave me tests, of which he shared the results. The results measured different aspects of me—prior to and after Dennis was arrested.
What the results indicated, the doctor said, was that right after Dennis' arrest I was suffering from Severe Traumatic Stress Disorder—what often is referred to as Post Traumatic Stress Syndrome.
The tests also measured my honesty, and the doctor said the tests, indeed, showed that I was being honest with him.
Every aspect of the tests measured normal except for the stress. I was prescribed a Beta Blocker to slow down my heart rate, as well as Prozac, and of course the weekly visits with the doctor.
During those visits, the doctor told me that I had a very heightened sixth sense, which could, of course, be a curse or a blessing. I told him that it was a curse. I can't tell you how many times in my life that I have had an

overwhelming gut feeling about something or someone, to only have not one person listen to me.

I felt like the character Chief Dan George played in the film *Little Big Man*. I'm talking about the scene in which cavalrymen are riding around killing Indians and Chief Dan George is walking unharmed through the melee and he says, "I've never been invisible before."

That's exactly how I felt.

Invisible.

And I'd had enough of that feeling.

One habit I picked up was at the urging of the doctor to come up with a positive, cheerful phrase to use as a parting comment at the end of phone calls, e-mails, and even in face to face encounters. I've found it helps me keep a positive attitude more consistently. It might seem silly to you, but it works for me. Here's the phrase:

Have a charming day.

For a while, to help myself lose my fears of being back out in public places, I started going to little auctions, mainly estate sales, and I learned to sell things on e-Bay. I was heavy into *Shabby Chic* items.

Anyway, one day I needed the smallest of nuts for a Tole Chandelier I stopped at a locally-owned hardware store in Park City, because I was short on time and couldn't make it to Home Depot.

Well, when I walked through the door the gentleman working there stopped in his tracks and asked me how in the heck I was doing. He went on and on about Dennis and Park City. I found out that he too had moved from Park City; he had had enough. He said, "I told my wife we're selling the house and getting the heck out of here."

I had crossed paths with this man during the course of my duties, and we got along just fine even when I was delivering bad news. Even back then he would bitch about Dennis and Jack. The man told me that day that I'd always treated him with respect in the course of doing my job. He appeared quite sincere.

Even before I started working for Park City this gentleman had installed a satellite dish in his front yard, and Jack hated that and would try all he could to get it removed. One time Jack directed me to send Mr. Perry a letter saying that he had to remove the satellite dish from his yard.

Well, I read over the city ordinances and could not find anything that would justify sending such a letter to Mr. Perry. The city ordinance was amended and the man had to remove the satellite dish.

So Mr. Perry moved.

Jack would every once in a while direct me to go do something that I thought was out of line, and which would have been a violation of the citizen's rights. I would never do it if I couldn't find anything in the ordinances to back it up. I mean, it was my butt on the line . . . and my signature on the letter.

I don't think Jack appreciated that; however, I'm sure the citizens did.

This reminds me of a time when Dennis sent me out to check on health and safety issues at an address. When I returned I informed him that I didn't see anything that would be out of line.

Dennis got hateful, and asked me if I got out of the truck and went into the back yard. I said, "No, there was a fence, and I could not see anything from the truck into the back yard that gave me cause to enter the back yard."

He said, "It is your job."

I said, "Not without cause, it isn't."

He got really pissed, and the heated argument was on. I told him that a person with a fence—whether privacy or chain link—has a reasonable expectation of privacy according to the Legal Aspects of Code Enforcement, and that for me to enter a yard to check in the backyard without seeing a violation from the curtilage would be a violation of their 4th Amendment rights.

That sent him over the edge considering I was not supposed to know more than him. He glared and, raising his voice, ordered, "Go back and check and yard!"

I responded, "I'm not getting sued! When the city gives me a Letter of Indemnification signed by the council members and the mayor that would hold me harmless, then I will go over and violate someone's rights!"

Later, I got the book out and marked the page for Dennis and put it in his in basket.

The next day Dennis told me he'd given it to Jack, and that Jack's reply was the same as his—that our city ordinance says that I can enter the yard without permission, but that they would talk to the city attorney about it.

I guess I don't have to tell you the outcome—I was right, and things changed after that. Citizens couldn't just call in and say that their neighbor's back yard looked like hell, and expect us to do something about it, unless they (the complainers) gave us permission to view it from their own back yard—and if it was a privacy fence, well, they were out of luck. We might make an exception if they lived in a two-story house that had a window that overlooked the backyard of the offending yard.

You see, you can't look through peepholes, stand on a ladder, so forth. It has to be in plain sight, and at an advantage point that would not be a violation of the person's 4th Amendment rights. The bottom line was that most citizens want to get along with their neighbors and, therefore, would many times say, "Just forget it," even though they were pissed off.

I don't think it ever stopped Dennis from doing what Dennis wanted, because people continued to complain about Dennis entering their yards without permission.

Just to set the record straight, Dennis was not the only Park City employee I filed a grievance about.

Back in 2000, while Dennis and I still shared the small office space, I was working one day at my desk while Dennis was taking his lunch break at home, as was his habit. I got up to go to the break room to get a Diet Pepsi. As I approached the entryway on the way back to our office, a city official was standing blocking my exit. He reached up and grabbed my pig tails and said, "Is these your love handles?"

I jerked loose and passed him and continued on my way. I told several people, including my husband Bob at the time, what this city official had said. Along with another girl that worked in the City Hall building—he'd been making suggestive comments to her—we filed grievances because of the man's actions. We gave our grievances to the mayor at the time, Olin Heibert.

A few days later the mayor spoke to me, and I couldn't believe my ears. He said, "Mary, don't you think you're overreacting?"

My understanding is that the mayor said the same thing to the other girl.

I mentioned it to Dee Stuart, who at the time was a council member. Her reply was almost identical to what the mayor had told me, and added, "He has such a nice wife; can't you imagine what this could do to her?"

Internally, I silently screamed, *WHAT THE HELL!!! My self-esteem, self-worth, and public standing is not equal to hers! Hey, I didn't marry him. That's her problem, not mine.*

My problem was his remark to me as well as touching me.

If you think things have improved at City Hall since I left and Dennis' real identity was exposed, think again. Two police officers that were president and vice-president for the Fraternal Order of Police were dismissed for giving a news statement regarding the treatment of employees in the Police Department, as well as over their own little hell regarding Park City government that was going on at the same time I was working with Mr. Evil.

These were good, honest, veteran officers that knew their job. But because they didn't keep their mouths shut and instead stood up to do the right thing, they were fired.

No, the situation has not improved; it's the same. Ask a city employee a question and you'll probably get a blank stare or a *no comment answer.* They will avoid you like the plague, especially if the question has anything to do with Mary Capps or Dennis Rader.

Just like I was, they are the remaining victims of Park City Hall. They have what they consider to be good jobs with insurance, vacation and sick pay, and are secure as long as they keep their mouths shut and don't talk about city business outside of the office.

Wouldn't it be great if we could get all the secrets these employees have? It sure would be enlightening.

The lawsuit that Tad, my attorney, filed vs. Jack Whitson and Dennis Rader eventually went to Federal court. The judge had no choice but to throw it out as, by then, the statute of limitations had expired.

It was never about money and never has been. Yes, Tad made some mistakes in filing my case; however, as soon as he realized that he might be in over his head, he found another attorney to assist us, but by this time it was in Federal court and time was up. Randy attempted to show cause for the judge to allow me to be heard, but the judge had to stand by the law; therefore

I lost my chance in court to hold the city accountable. Randy told me that he had to advise me that I could appeal the decision, or I could sue Tad, or move on with my life.

I chose to write this book telling the truth, and I also told Randy that Tad was a good person and that no way in hell would I sue him . . . for what . . . for money?

It was never about the money.

In December 2006, my family (aunts uncles, cousins, my fiancé Jim and I, Mom and Dad, sisters) went to dinner at a local restaurant. One of my aunts told me that Dee Stuart, who was now the mayor of Park City, told her to pass on a message to me. The message was that I should sue my attorney. I asked my aunt to return this message:

IT'S NOT ABOUT MONEY:
IT'S ABOUT THE TRUTH!

Upon reflection about something Dee had told me previously, I realized that it must be just a money situation for her. Right after she was elected in 2005, she had told my dad that I should sell my story to one of the tabloids.

When I heard that I thought, *What the Hell . . . and lose my credibility?*

I just wanted my story told before a jury to hold the city accountable. I didn't care if my attorney or the city attorneys made a lot of money from my case. Hell, I hoped they did. All I wanted was justice—that for me is riches.

What the Park City government never seemed to grasp was that I filed my lawsuit against them *only* to hold them accountable for the harassment I received from Dennis Rader—not BTK. The sad thing is that if he had never been found to be BTK, I would never have had the platform for my voice to be heard. And because he was found to be BTK, they got shoved into the arena of attention.

Forty-one: Fighting City Hall

So here we are:

The entire world knows Dennis Rader as BTK, and about the horrible things that he did.

He murdered women, children, and one man, as well as attempted to murder another man.

He impersonated other people in his endeavors to accomplish this.

He stole from the dead victims.

He mentally tortured surviving young children.

He lied, cheated and stole from his employers, including his last employer—Park City.

Despite all of this and the testimony from the police, as well as in his own words, that he did these things; also, in his own words, that Park City officials were too busy to watch him—all of this, and the city government stood by him.

For six and one-half years I complained about Dennis Rader and his treatment directed at me, as well as complained that it was unfair to file my grievances with my immediate supervisor, which was the one I was complaining about.

So after his arrest, I along with other employees from the Police Department, as well as my Aunt Janice, attempted to get the city government to change the policy regarding the grievance filing process.

My aunt attended every city council meeting, as did my daughter and sister, Kim. I attended a couple council meetings myself, but for the most part I was still keeping a low profile in public.

I remember attending one specific meeting because the grievance policy was on the agenda. I signed in at the front so I could address City Council before they took it to a vote. I still saw problems with what they were proposing because it still required that you take it to your immediate supervisor first.

Recently-elected Mayor Dee Stuart, who got elected largely through my family's support, approached me and told me that I wouldn't be able to address City Council on the matter. I told her that since I was still employed, yes, I could.

Dee replied that they were taking it off of the agenda.

I answered that I would then speak during Public Forum.

She walked off.

The news media was present. The meeting was called to order, and the council members started making changes to the agenda, but they didn't move to take off the grievance policy.

I thought it was pretty sneaky of them to do it that way. If there is an item listed on the agenda, then we weren't allowed to address it during Public Forum. This meant that when it went to Public Forum, I was not allowed to speak.

After Public Forum, you want to guess what they did?

Right. You got it.

They made a motion to remove the grievance policy from the agenda.

To say that I was pissed would be the all-time under-statement. After all these years I never had a voice and still didn't. I hated those people for their own lack of empathy.

I got up and approached a news reporter. We went outside and I read the same statement that I had planned to read to the council—which was what I thought about the grievance policy.

After Dennis was arrested, I stayed employed with Park City until after his sentencing on August 18—almost six full months. Except for two weeks' paid vacation, I was off without pay throughout that entire time. As a matter of fact, I never received unemployment, sick pay, or disability consideration due to me being diagnosed as having Post Traumatic Stress Syndrome. I had no income whatsoever.

I never sold a story. NOTHING. And there were plenty of opportunities, especially with the tabloids who had representatives all over the place.

You want to know the amount of the advance I got to write this book?

The answer will surprise you.

No money crossed my palm.

What I got was the promise that my story would be told. And that promise was kept. Yes, I will make a percentage of any resulting profits, and that is very fair.

I have never asked for pity and I never will. I'm just stating facts for those people that thought I was receiving some type of compensation.

But, as I was saying, I was still employed. After the sentencing hearing I made an appointment to see Jack Whitson. I wanted to find out if my employee annual reviews were going to be removed from my files.

Jack said, "No."

He said that should I return to work, I would be placed on probation for six months, and after that I would be given the chance for a new review.

CAN YOU BELIEVE THIS CRAP?

I couldn't.

Dennis, although he was a lair and a murderer, and cheat and thief—the Park City government accepted what he said as truth regarding my reviews.

A serial killer's word was better than mine.

I wanted to hit something.

I wanted to scream.

Anything.

Something.

Well, I severed my employment with Park City. The City of Park City is a wonderful town with wonderful people, some of whom were victims of Dennis Rader's manipulation.

But the city government lacks in empathy.

Just like Dennis Rader did.

Postscript

Life is good.

As I write this I am about to go out riding on Harleys with Jim Mies, my fiancé.

My sense of humor is back. In fact, I'm smiling right now, thinking of a comment a friend made just yesterday.

Do you know what they call people that ride motorcycles at your age?
Donor.

I love the feel of the wind blowing my hair, and the awesome power of the Harley beneath me. It's just an experience you have to have to fully appreciate what I'm saying.

I'm happy with my appearance, and am told often that I'm attractive. I have dark green eyes, large as well; a nose that I am quite pleased with; and some freckles (they really show during the summer).

I wear little to no makeup. My sister and daughter tell me all the time that I am one of the lucky ones that do not have to wear makeup.

One habit that virtually disappeared while I was working for Park City is back:

Once again I'm stopping to smell the roses.

I see animal shapes in the clouds, and I daydream.

I've been spending time with my grandchildren, who were 7, 6, and 3 when I wrote this postscript.

One day before the weather got colder I was sitting outside watching my two oldest grandchildren playing with the herd of neighborhood children.

I smiled and couldn't stop smiling as memories flooded back of all the happy, fun times I enjoyed as a child.

At the begging request of my granddaughter I passed out Popsicles to the neighborhood kids, and as I looked into the dirty faces of these children, at how very happy they were doing the same things we did as children— they didn't have their GameBoys with them; no, they had their bicycles, dolls, trucks, and were climbing trees—I began to wonder:

Do things really come full circle, and will my grand-children remember these times as fondly as I do my childhood?

Welcome to the world of MarJim Books, publisher of books bearing the UCS PRESS imprint.

Sure, we publish crime books—watch for ***Winnie Ruth Judd: The Trunk Murders Classic*** in October 2007, and for the April 2008 release of an investigative book about the mysterious death of an international celebrity—but crime books do not begin to define all of who we are.

UCS PRESS launched in 1987 with the publication of Dr. Larry Waldman's popular ***Who's Raising Whom? A Parent's Guide to Effective Child Discipline.***

We're pleased to report that this book, plus three other Dr. Waldman titles, will be released later in 2007 under the UCS PRESS imprint, including:

Coping with your adolescent
How come I love him but can't live with him?
Blended Families: They're All Mixed Up

Dr. Waldman is known for his ability to explain why children, teenagers, and married adults do what they do that drives parents and spouses up the wall—and to offer solutions that really work if applied.

The cutting-edge ***Arresting The Great Mind-Robber: Commonsense approaches to Alzheimer's*** by independent researcher James F. Watson also will be released later in 2007. His companion book—***Sandy: My magnificent obsession***—is in development.

The latter book is an amazing true love story. When Watson's wife began showing symptoms of Alzheimer's Disease, he literally put his business life on hold and became a self-taught neuroscientist so that he could discover the many causes of Alzheimer's. When he succeeded in achieving this goal, he set his next goal, which was to find a way to reverse the Alzheimer's symptoms his wife was displaying. And when he succeeded in achieving that goal, he knew he had to tell the world what he had learned. That is when he wrote **Arresting The Great Mind-Robber.**

Two inspirational books are in development:

Walking on the Dead by Sim Taing with Jim Dobkins

He made moccasins by Bill Mulgrew with Jim Dobkins.

Sim Taing was a boy of five when Pol Pot, in 1975, began the systematic slaughter of one-third of Cambodia's population. From the innocent viewpoint of a young boy, who advances in age from five to nine, this gripping true story is told. The title derives from an incident when Sim's family had escaped from Cambodia into Thailand only to be forced at machine-gun point to go back into Cambodia across a large minefield. Sim survived by walking on the bodies of dead people killed by the exploding mines.

Bill Mulgrew is a man of intense faith, who has experienced what many people would call miracles. And one of the miracles is that he has the medical documents to back up what he says. The title for this book was inspired by a true event. Bill had been in Florida and somehow had contracted gangrene that was advancing up both of his legs. He was transported to the Veteran's Hospital in Phoenix, Arizona not far from his home in Mesa, Arizona.

Surgery was scheduled to amputate a portion of both legs close to his knees to stop the advance of the skin-rotting gangrene. A prostheses technician was sent to Bill's hospital room. The man had a variety of leather pieces from which, he told Bill, he would form temporary stump covers after Bill was returned to his room from recovery. The technician left. When they came to take Bill to surgery, he was sitting on the edge of his bed, having just made moccasins for *both* feet from the leather scraps. They thought he was crazy. Bill was taken to surgery, and then he asked everyone to leave the room so he could be alone for a few minutes. They left. He prayed. When they returned there was no sign of the gangrene. Bill still wears the moccasins today.

Also in development for release later in 2007 is a wonderfully creative, unique children's storybook: **The Little Sleepies Reader.** It's from the amazing mind of Bob Childs, a retiree who was a member of Seal Team Two way back when. Bob is an unusually gifted storyteller. For now, we won't give away any of his plot lines; however, we will tell you this: **The Little Sleepies Reader** is as originally creative as *Monsters, Inc., Shrek*, and *Chicken Run*. The stories are that captivating. If you have young children or grandchildren, they—and you—will absolutely love **The Little Sleepies**.

Winnie Ruth Judd: The Trunk Murders Classic is a re-release of *Winnie Ruth Judd: The Trunk Murders* by J. Dwight Dobkins and Robert J. Hendricks. It originally was released by Grosset & Dunlap in 1973, enjoyed an 18-month run in the Doubleday Bargain Book Club, and was optioned six times as a possible film. That book established Dobkins and Hendricks as the experts on the notorious "Trunk Murders" case.

The publicist for Grosset & Dunlap wrote, "Two crack journalists have unearthed the incredible facts involving the most astonishing crime of the century." Attempting to describe why this was "the crime of passion that stunned a nation," the publisher's news release touched on some of the issues that this first comprehensive book about the case would address:

Phoenix, Arizona in 1931 was the scene of this grisly murder...the gruesome remains of two women were discovered in trunks leaking blood. The slayer proved to be none other than their friend, Winnie Ruth Judd—The Tiger Woman...as she was referred to in headlines across the country. Mysteries involving the case were whispered about for decades. What made Winnie do it? Was she involved with an "accomplice," a rich Phoenix businessman...? How did she manage to cop an insanity plea, spending 34 years in jail and a mental institution instead of facing the hangman's noose?

Here are the answers—plus all her hair-raising escapes, sensational trials and last strange recapture years later, involving another brutal, still unsolved murder.

Other books set for release by UCS PRESS include:

Dr. Sally's Voodoo Man, a brilliant first novel by Mary Hanford Bruce. This is the debut book in the Dr. Sally series.

Right Crosses, the dramatic story of Adar and Molid, the thieves who died on crosses flanking Jesus' cross, by Jim Dobkins and Stephanie Childs. This historical novel captures well the tragic events of 1st century Palestine.

Buy UCS PRESS titles at www.marjimbooks.com.